© 2023 by Susan L. Atchison

All rights reserved. No part of this book may be reproduced, stored in a retrieval system, or transmitted by any means without the express written permission of the editor.

Printed in the United States of America

Published by Susan L. Atchison, 2023

ISBN: 979-8-9876594-0-3

All photos included in this book are copyrighted solely by the credited artist.

Loving Insights

A Higher Perspective on Emotions

Susan L. Atchison, LCPC

To the Light

May it glow, grow, and flow within and between everyone on Earth.
May all beings on Earth know the Light, feel the Light, be the Light,
and share the Light.
May there be peace on Earth—peace, peace, and perfect peace.

Table of Contents

Introduction 1

About the Lotus Flower Symbol 5

Emotions 7
    Acceptance 9
    Anger 15
    Anxiety 19
    Avoidance 25
    Belonging 29
    Betrayal 33
    Bitterness 37
    Bliss 41
    Compassion 45
    Criticism 49
    Depression 53
    Despair 59
    Determination 63
    Disappointment 67
    Empathy 71
    Emptiness 75
    Faith 79
    Fear 83
    Forgiveness 87
    Fulfillment 91
    Gratitude 95
    Greed 99
    Grief 103
    Guilt 107
    Hopelessness 111
    Impatience 117
    Inspiration 121
    Jealousy 125
    Joy 129
    Judgment 133
    Laziness 139
    Loneliness 145

Emotions (continued)

Love 149
Numbness 153
Oneness 157
Rage 161
Rebelliousness 165
Rejection 169
Resentment 173
Sadness 177
Self-Empowerment 181
Shame 187
Shock 191
Worthiness 195

Recommended Resources 199

Photo Credits 203

Acknowledgments 211

About the Author 215

Personalized Loving Insights Message 216

Introduction

Emotions. We all have them. When you reflect on situations in your life, while you may recall the people, activities, or surroundings, usually it is the emotion associated with them that make them memorable. Emotions color our lives, and emotions are what anchor memories into our brains—and bodies.

We all may have different experiences in life, but all people have many of the same or similar emotions, even the "difficult" ones. We are human, and as such, we are given the challenge or gift—depending on how you look at it—of the range of emotional states.

As a counselor, my calling is to help people with their emotions, so thinking about and working with emotions is a big part of my life. And then there are my own emotions. One of my therapy teachers said, "You can't take someone somewhere you haven't been." This means that, in my own therapy sessions, I've had to bring up, look at, and work through lots of emotions. Some were easier, some were harder, and some were… well, much, much harder. Some still are hard. This journey continues—it is a lifelong one.

Alongside my emotional journey has been my spiritual journey. It seems that I am always working on one or the other—or both together. Spirituality and emotions are intricately intertwined. They are bound together. We need to dive down into our most difficult emotions to progress upward on our spiritual journey. Otherwise, the weight of heavy emotions will keep us from rising up in our spiritual consciousness. We can only go as high as we have gone low.

As I worked through and released my own emotions, my intuition began to unfold. What a gift this was! I often had envied the people around me who had strong intuitive, even psychic, abilities. They would tell me that anyone could develop intuition, but I didn't believe them. My mind seemed to be stuck in the linear world. Finally, after years of effort—or maybe it was that it simply took years for me to believe I could let go of the "efforting"—my mind began to open to new wisdom and insights from a higher perspective and to guidance from the higher realms.

Because the words that came were always based in love, I call this wisdom "Loving Insights." These Loving Insights come from a consciousness that resides in a higher, more heavenly world where things are different than they are on Earth. This is acknowledged and reflected when a Loving Insights reading uses a phrase, such as, "In your world."

As I began to explore the new wisdom that came with this expanded intuition, it seemed natural to focus it on emotions. If a client requests it, I can bring forth a Loving Insights message for them. The messages are always a reminder of that person's intrinsic beauty, value, and worth. These have proved to be very meaningful to my clients—several of them have told me that they keep their Loving Insights messages on their bedside table or all together in a folder. One client even framed her message.

My teachers emphasized that when we learn something, we need to share it with others. This is the flow of life. It also is an innate drive in me—I love to pass along to others what I've learned. As such, this book was born to share with others a higher, more loving perspective on emotions.

While writing these Loving Insights intuitive messages, I got to take another tour through the landscape of emotions. As each topic came up in my consciousness and I prepared to write about it, I realized, "I've got that!" Yes, I've got difficult emotions, such as judgment, resentment, greed—you name it. That is humbling to say the least. But I also have the good ones like inspiration, patience, and self-empowerment. We ALL do.

I like to call the difficult emotions the "learning emotions." We have them, and sometimes are stuck in them because we are learning something from them. Once that lesson is completed, typically they don't bother us so much anymore. While we are in that learning phase, we can take power away from the difficult emotional states by acknowledging them. Is that counterintuitive?

You've probably heard the phrase, "What you resist, persists." When we acknowledge something, that very acknowledgment opens the door for it to dissipate. If you want, you can go one step further and honor that state. After all, it probably is trying to accomplish something for you. It might not always be in the most productive way—imagine a toddler pouring an entire box of soap bubbles in the washing machine because she wants to help her mommy wash clothes—but underneath the action, the intention usually is to help. Often the focus of that help is to protect you in some way. If you feel like you can go even one more step, we can love all our emotional states like we would love the toddler—although not her behavior at that moment! We love her desire to help, and we love her essence.

Our "learning" experiences also can be viewed like the manure that grows the garden of our lives. The lotus flower is a prime example of that. This beautiful flower only can grow when its roots are in muck and mud. From that yucky place comes radiant beauty. That's what the cover of this book depicts. May you find this book helpful to you as you travel your own journey of life.

Chapter Organization

This book covers 44 emotions. Some, like self-empowerment, are more a state of being than an emotion, but for simplicity's sake, they all are referred to in this book as emotions. Each emotion has three sections:

1. **Personal Reflections.** This is a brief introductory discussion of the emotion. Sometimes I use examples of how it has been experienced in my life or in the lives of others, and sometimes I'm just wondering about the emotion.
2. **Loving Insights.** This is the intuitive wisdom, or higher perspective, given for that emotion.
3. **Inspired Actions: Tips and Tools for Transformation.** This is what you can do to bring that emotional state into balance. In this section, I offer a variety of easy yet effective techniques. I believe there is wisdom in many different faiths and practices, so you'll find some techniques from Christianity, Buddhism, Hinduism, and so forth. You do not need to believe in these faiths to benefit from the exercises. Truth, love, forgiveness, and compassion essentially are the same across different faiths.

The Intent

This book is not meant to be read cover to cover. You may find it best to read just one or two sections at a time so you can then process them or practice the suggestions given. Or you may use the book in a "devotional" way—picking it up and letting it open to a "random" page that can be your focus, message, or devotion for the day.

My hope is that this book will give you a new understanding of some of the challenges, lessons, and joys in life. Sometimes what the Loving Insights says is an affirmation of wisdom that is already in the world, and sometimes it is new—to me at least.

Ultimately, as the old saying goes, there probably is not much new under the Sun, but I have found that guidance given in the right words and at the right time can make a positive difference or impact. May that be so for you.

About the Lotus Flower Symbol

*To heal, you have to get to the root of the wound
and kiss it all the way up.*
— Rupi Kaur, author and poet —

A lotus plant only can grow when its roots are in muck. The lotus grows up through the water toward the Sun to blossom in a most beautiful and radiant way. Our lives are like that, too. Often, we begin rooted in something yucky or mucky, then we grow through the water (an element representing emotions). Once we have reached the Light, we blossom in our own beautiful and radiant way.

The lotus flower provides us with several levels of symbolism. When the lotus is not yet in bloom, it represents the potential for something to blossom in your life. In Sanskrit, the lotus is called *pankaj*, which means "born of mud." This reminds those of us who are focused on growing out of our lower emotions to continue that growth toward a lighter sense of being. And we have help on this journey. The stem of the lotus flower is said to be Mother Divine: She who helps us grow out of the mud of worldly emotions.

The lotus flower submerges into the water each night and miraculously reemerges and blooms each morning. We can think of this as cleansing and rebirth, or our process of going into the subconscious while we sleep each night, to then awake refreshed and renewed in the morning.

You will find a line drawing of a lotus plant in the section on Acceptance. Use this image to write in words reflecting your own journey from the mucky, yucky beginning through the growth path that you took up through the watery emotional field, noting the resources that help support you and the qualities that blossomed in your life as a result of the growth.

To get a free template of the lotus flower, go to www.lovinginsights.com. Put the Acceptance section in your cart then use the coupon code LOTUS to download it for free.

When you're done writing down your journey, you may want to color in the picture.

Loving Insights Emotions

Susan L. Atchison

Acceptance

*Life is a series of natural and spontaneous changes.
Don't resist them; that only creates sorrow. Let reality be reality.
Let things flow naturally forward in whatever way they like.*
— Lao Tzu —

Personal Reflections

Acceptance seems like a double-edged sword to me.

On one hand, accepting "what is" is said to take away the angst of not having something we want (like better finances) or having something we don't want (like a poor health condition). Taking away the angst can bring you peace of mind.

The term "radical acceptance" is based on accepting that sometimes life brings you situations that feel painful and can seem unfair. Radical acceptance suggests that if you accept that this is part of life, you may still have the pain, but you do not have to suffer by ruminating about it. Proving that there are no new thoughts under the Sun, Lao Tzu said the same thing 2,500 years ago (see the quote at the beginning of this section).

Does this mean that we should just accept a less-than-positive situation? Does a battered spouse just accept that this is the way it is? Does the person who is enduring discrimination just accept that? Also, aren't we taught to set goals, do affirmations, and visualize the experiences we want to have? Should we just accept that we do not have the mate, job, finances, health, or life that we want?

It can be confusing. I need a higher perspective on this.

Loving Insights

Beloved child of the Universe, indeed, this topic is one of great complexity for you. The true meaning of acceptance is to know that you are in the flow of God's divine plan. When you accept what is (such as with the loss of a spouse), you begin to look for the positive reasonings this experience might bring to you. This can lessen your grief and help you move forward.

When you want to set goals and envision a different way of being, or different set of emotions, you are in the process of accepting that things will be changing for you. Truthfully, you can't step in the same stream twice; things are always changing for you whether you know it or not. When you put your children to bed at night, you may not notice that they are taller or bigger in the morning, but they are. You just haven't noticed it yet. At what point does the awareness that things are different begin to kick in?

You can accept that you are always, always, always on your way to a different experience. You can accept that God is always, always, always giving you unconditional love, peace, and harmony. Dig down in yourself to this level of awareness and acceptance and you will no longer be confused. Acceptance becomes all there is.

Me: Let me see if I understand. The person who just lost a spouse can accept that she has grief, that she will struggle, that she will learn, and that she will grow?

Loving Insights: Yes, that's right.

Me: Then the person who is being abused, what does he accept?

LI: He accepts that he will know the exact right time and the exact right way to move away from this situation, that God is right now orchestrating events and people to bring a new way of life to him and free him from these earthly shackles.

Me: So, should this person take action or steps to improve his life?

LI: Absolutely. Those action steps are part of his acceptance that God is bringing him a better way.

Inspired Actions: Tips and Tools for Transformation

Tips

Maybe acceptance actually is the beginning of change. If we are not accepting of a situation, then we are using a lot of mental energy protesting or arguing with, or about, that situation. Doesn't that just keep us wrapped up, or trapped in, the situation? Once we accept the reality of it, we can let go of all the unproductive mental energy, which frees us up to be open to new ideas and resources that actually can begin to change the situation.

Tools

When bringing something into balance, it is helpful to have both words and actions.

Words, such as those used in affirmations, state our intentions and send them out into the Universe as well as inward to our own subconscious:

> I accept that all is in Divine Order; I accept that God wants the highest good for me, and I accept that this is being orchestrated and brought to me in the perfect right way. I accept that I am worthy of this love and care from the highest level, and I accept my right to receive it.

Actions take the energies of our intentions and begin to bring them into manifestation. You can use the easy lotus blossom art therapy technique that follows as an action to begin your manifestation.

Lotus seeds sprout and begin to grow roots only in muck and mud. They NEED that muck and mud in order to grow upward and then blossom into their luminous flowers. They are a perfect metaphor for our lives.

Using the line drawing that follows as an example, draw a lotus flower. If you don't want to draw your own, feel free to photocopy the blank line drawing at the end of this section. You also can download a print of the drawing from www.lovinginsights.com. Select the Acceptance section on the website to put it in your cart then use the coupon code LOTUS to download it for free.

An example is shown to help you envision how it is done. Whether you draw your own lotus or use the line drawing in this book, write in your own words based on your personal experiences.

- On the roots, write words that describe what created or contributed to your difficult situation or what is making you struggle. That's the muck in which the seeds of your life were planted.
- The stem is the path that you took or are taking, so write along the stem what has helped, or is helping, you grow.
- The leaves represent what has helped or is helping support you.
- The flower petals are what has blossomed in your life through this process.

Emotions: Acceptance

Once you have reflected on your personal words and actions, you will see how acceptance of what is will help you move forward and grow.

Example of the lotus with words written in:

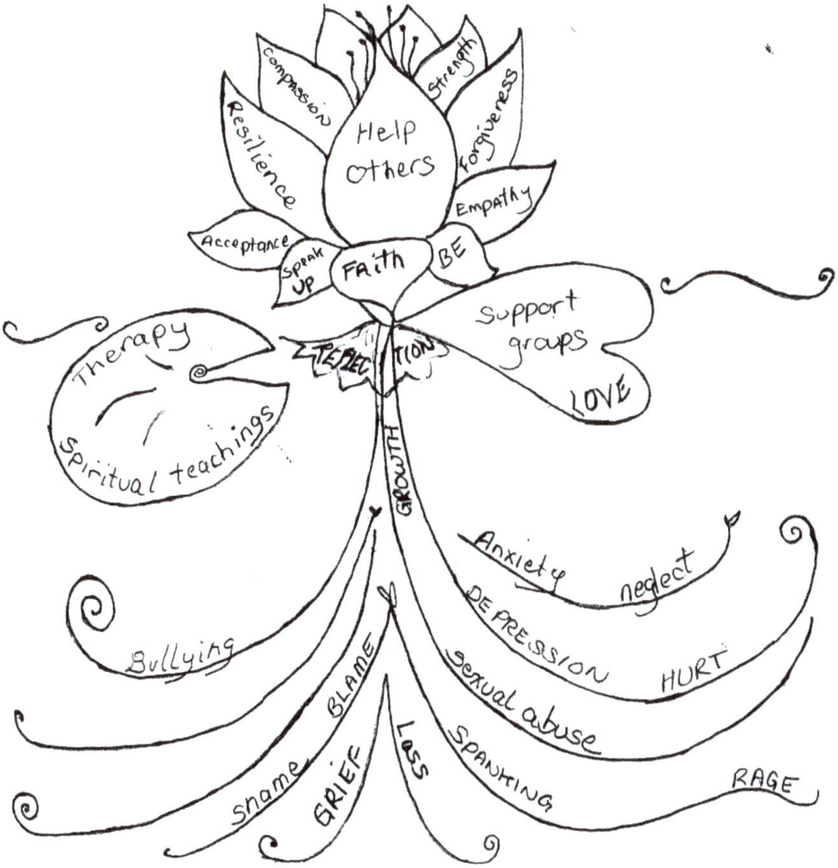

Here is a blank lotus for you to fill in with your own words.

You can photocopy this page or download an original copy from www.lovinginsights.com. Select the Acceptance section on the website to put it in your cart then use the coupon code LOTUS to download it for free.

Anger

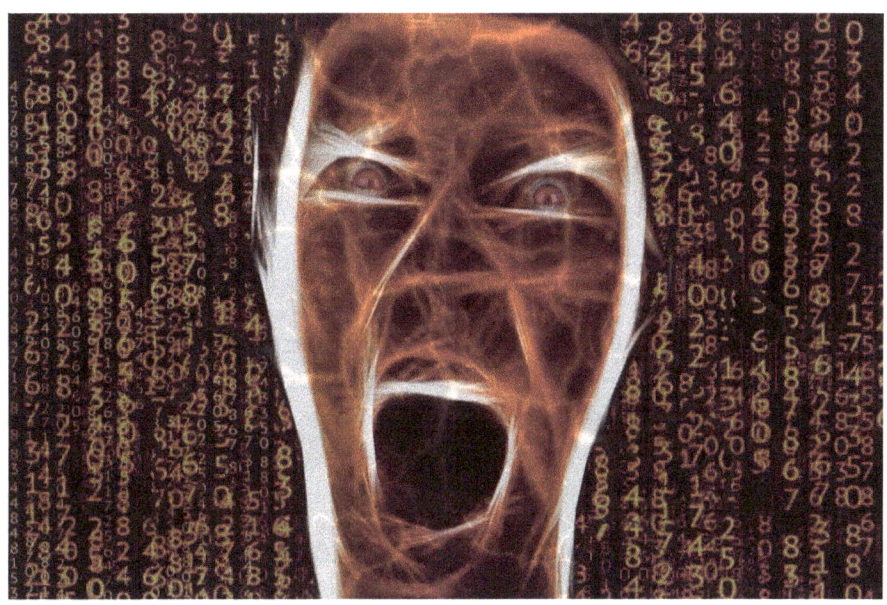

*Do not teach your children never to be angry;
teach them how to be angry.*
— Lyman Abbott —

Personal Reflections

Anger can be thought of as existing on a continuum, from very much to very little. On one end, sometimes we have too much anger—such as when we get angry at other drivers. On the other end, sometimes our anger is repressed, and we do not acknowledge it. But if you squish something too tightly, its contents eventually will find a way out. For example, if you put too much water in a balloon and then squeeze it, the balloon will burst, and the water will shoot out. Sometimes our anger is like that.

I know this from personal experience. My father was angry, and so was the grandmother with whom we lived. It was a lot of anger to live with as a child. Part of me would like to think that being around their anger helped me learn not to be angry and to find another way. But instead, my response was to push my own anger down. Of course, it didn't STAY down. It came out most often as irritation (which a colleague wisely once referred to as "rage leaking out of a little hole"). It took a lot of concerted attention and effort over many years to defuse that irritation/anger.

Loving Insights

Most holy ones, people with anger are often portrayed in the world's art as having flames coming out of their heads. This is very apt symbolism because anger truly is an intense inflammation of the emotions. Think of physical inflammation; it is helpful when used in its intended way—to bring healing resources to an injured area of the body—but it is not helpful when it continues to flow unabated. The same applies to emotional anger; it can be a strength and a tool when used correctly. The proper use of anger is to mindfully move one out of a negative, dangerous, or unhelpful situation.

Unfortunately, people have grasped onto anger and given it a home in their heads and their hearts. Much of the world now is run on anger. This is inflammation run amok. It will burn out the world as surely as unchecked physical inflammation will burn out the body. Just like people can be unaware of high blood pressure or chronic inflammation until the symptoms become quite severe, so too are people often unaware of the dangers of chronic anger.

Do not think you cannot make an impact on the world's anger. You are the only one who can! Each time you choose to react mindfully rather than angrily, you lighten the world's inflammation. If you choose to be angry at someone, that can "fire up" the other person up so he or she takes their anger out on someone or something else. Instead, you can have a positive impact when you breathe through the incipient anger. The peace and calmness you bring yourself will be felt by those around you, and they will, in turn, bring that peace and calmness to others. Imagine how far this can spread.

Decide today. Will anger be the main tool in your toolbox, or will you reach for more elevated ones?

Inspired Actions: Tips and Tools for Transformation

Tips

Think about the kinds of situations in which you tend to feel anger. Is there a pattern in these situations? This will help you prepare to experience anger in a different way.

How do you know the proper use of anger? Train yourself to pause and ask these questions:

- Is this anger mine?
- Is the anger due to something happening right now, or is it being triggered by unresolved residual emotions from past events?
- Is there another way I can resolve this issue without resorting to anger?

Pay attention to your body's reactions. Notice your breathing as you ask yourself these questions. A true answer will be signified by a naturally deep breath and a full exhale.

Tools

Each night, do a reverse review of that day. Mentally go through your feelings, words, and actions from evening through morning. If you felt, said, or did something in anger, feel that in your body. Now be kind to yourself. It is likely you were running on subconscious programming. Unwind the reel of that event to the beginning then acknowledge the part of you that got angry. Help that part feel safe. Often, we feel anger because we are scared or don't feel safe. Tell that part, "You are safe now; it's okay."

Then ask for your guides to give you whatever resources you need to truly feel safe. You might think of someone you know who handles situations like yours with a more positive attitude. If you don't have a person in your life like this, you can look to anyone who is calm and wise, such as a spiritual leader like the Pope or the Dalai Lama, or even a character from a book, TV show, or movie. This person can be your mentor.

Now, redo that event. In your mind, take yourself through it, but this time experience it in a more positive way. If you feel that anger still coming up, breathe into it. Feel, see, sense, or know that light is coming in and diffusing it. Bring in your "mentor," if you need her or him, to coach you on how to do this more effectively. You might envision her or him standing with you, helping you breathe, helping you feel safe, and helping you respond more appropriately. Once you have re-envisioned the event in a positive way, notice how your body feels. Acknowledge the great change you just made. If you were unable to totally change your response, accept that it's just not time yet. You made a start and that's good. You will try again tomorrow.

Anxiety

*Our anxiety does not empty tomorrow of its sorrows
but only empties today of its strengths.*
— Charles Haddon Spurgeon —

Personal Reflections

Anxiety. Who doesn't have it? We are anxious about our physical safety, about politics, money, sex, relationships, our jobs… you name it.

We have many different types of anxiety. There is anxiety from catastrophic thinking: "The Russians are coming!" There is situational anxiety, such as being in a job interview. Then there is more subtle, continual anxiety: "Did I say the right thing? What if she didn't like me?" Some people have so much anxiety, so often and about so many things, that psychologists have a name for it: "generalized anxiety."

Some years ago, I was going through an intense period of anxiety about whether I had made a mistake and said and done things that could hurt another or boomerang back and hurt me. In an attempt to neutralize that, I would focus really hard on transforming the anxiety about whatever it was I felt I had said or done "wrong." It would work (for a couple of minutes), then a new anxiety about something else would roll in.

As I thought about this process, I got the image of a soft drink vending machine. After putting the money in (my affirmation or whatever I was using to transform the situational anxiety), I pulled a "can" of anxiety about something out of the machine. With one fewer cans of anxiety in the machine, my anxiety load was lightened for a moment. But then the next can of anxiety just rolled down to take its place. That's when I realized that my anxiety wasn't reflective of any particular situation; it was about overall anxiety looking for something to focus on. That was an interesting concept, that I was not anxious about a particular situation, but rather the situation was giving my already-existing anxiety something to attach to.

Regardless of what kind it is or where it comes from, anxiety grabs hold of us and sometimes won't let go. It tightens our shoulders, shortens our breaths, ties our stomach in knots, and saps our energy. It really can take the fun out of life.

Loving Insights

Blessed ones, anxiety is like an undetected, subclinical infection that affects everything in your system. You feel anxiety in your very bones. Anxiety, once having taken up residence, tends to breed and expand over time. It is a toxin, a poison that must be rooted out and purged from your being. Anxiety takes the joy out of your life, and that is not acceptable. The Creator has designated that you live your lives in joy, peace, and contentment.

Listen to yourself. Really listen to the words being broadcast by your internal radio system. Would you listen to a cable show that continually told you that disaster was imminent, that you are not going to get your desires, that you are a screw-up? You would change the channel or even block that channel from your home. Well, your body and mind are your internal home. You need to take actions to keep it harmonious.

We understand that this is much, much easier said than done. So, start here. Pause for a moment. Is what you are anxious about happening right now? If yes, ask for help and take an action to begin to move through it. If no, is there anything you can do about it? If there is, take that action. If there is no action to be taken, bring your attention to your inner self. You are safe. You are safe. You are safe. Find that sweet spot deep inside where you are indeed safe. Breathe outward from that spot. Let that beautiful breath flow all through you. Be in this moment only. Feel your body begin to let go of the tension. You are safe. You are safe. You are safe.

Inspired Actions: Tips and Tools for Transformation

Tips

If anxiety is like a low-level infection, consider what your body might need if it had that same low-level infection. It would need more rest, fluids, and care, then it would need some detoxification. How can you take care of your body while you are helping your brain learn a way other than anxiety? Take in fluids and exercise to burn away the toxins.

When I've had repetitive anxious thoughts—my brain especially likes to play that game when I lie down to sleep—I've found relief by saying to myself, "I choose peace. I choose peace. I choose peace." It's hard to have more than one thought at a time, so I fill my mind with "I choose peace."

Tools

You can use your breaths to calm yourself down. Your body has two overall types of processes:

1. The autonomic nervous system—parts like your heart, circulation, digestion, and breathing—works without conscious control.
2. The voluntary muscle system—parts like your muscles and your breaths—encompasses what you can control.

Notice that your breath is part of both systems. It is the only one that is both conscious and unconscious, which makes it the link between the two!

By slowing your breathing, you can slow your body's other functions. One classic yogic pranayama (breathing) exercise is called "Left Nostril Breathing." You close off your right nostril with your thumb, then you inhale through the left nostril. Then, still keeping the right nostril closed, exhale only through the left nostril. Repeat this about 10 times.

Following are some simple yet surprisingly calming physical techniques you can use:

- Tap on your chin with one of your fingers. Try it—it's surprisingly calming.

- Press your thumb into the palm of the other hand and hold it there for a while.

- Place the palm of your hand over your forehead like someone does when they've just received a shock. The body does this intuitively because it creates a calming sensation. With your hand on your forehead, allow yourself to feel safe, held, and supported. If you'd like, put your other palm on the back of your head at the base of your skull as though you are cradling your head.

If you have a large reservoir of anxiety—such as the kind in which you are anxious all the time about nothing in particular and it repetitively attaches to any available situation—then you may wish to go deeper to transform it.

Often our anxiety comes from times in our childhood when either we were not nurtured enough or we were hurt in some way. We never learned to feel safe. Sit quietly and connect with that "inner child" who is not feeling safe. Let them tell you how they feel. Don't interpret, judge, or "fix" it. Just let them share then ask them what they need. Often it is just a hug. Give your inner child whatever they need and assure them they are safe. When they feel completely safe, you may wish to ask if they would like to move into your heart. Prepare a place in your heart with whatever your child likes—you might make a playground, a beautiful bedroom, or just a sort of nest. You can make sure there is a teddy bear, a favorite pet, or whatever they want or need. Then feel your child snuggle into this warm, safe place.

You are safe.

Susan L. Atchison

Avoidance

*Emotional pain cannot kill you but running from it can.
Allow. Embrace. Let yourself feel. Let yourself heal.*
— Vironika Tugaleva —

Personal Reflections

While writing this book, I often found just about anything else to do other than sitting down to work on it. It's funny how housework or other chores suddenly become necessary, or even inspiring, when there is something else we should be doing. When I shared this with a writer friend, she suggested that I include avoidance as a topic and that I put it first in the book! I said that I would get right on that. But I didn't. You got it—this is one of the last sections I finished.

Loving Insights

Beautiful ones, you see that human life is full of distractions and ways around the true work you should be doing, yet avoidance may have a purpose for showing up in your life.

Avoidance can happen when you are not yet in 100% alignment with your purpose. Avoidance also can be interpreted as an inner knowing that the time is not right yet. Then patience is a virtue. In these cases, you are well served by paying attention to your intuition. Listen to your body, which will tell you when it is ready to move and when it wants to stay in place.

Avoidance also can be a manifestation of the fear that you will not be safe if you complete a particular task. It is the fear that your life will change and change irrevocably.

Even if that change is for the good, it is human nature to want things to remain the same. When things remain the same, you do not have to think about them much or acclimate yourself to a new way of being. However, even though you think things are the same, they never are. Each day, each hour, and each moment is different and new. Therefore, you might as well get down to the business at hand, whether it is to do your homework, handle the chores, or write that book. Your only concern should be, "Will I be able to handle my life when this is done?" Yes, you will. And you may be surprised at how well you are able to handle it, but you will never know until you move into that point in time.

Inspired Actions: Tips and Tools for Transformation

Tips

When we understand that change is happening regardless of what we do or don't do, we can better understand that NOT making a decision actually IS making a decision. Similarly, not taking an action is taking an action.

Tools

Once you have determined that you are in alignment with what you want (and the time is right), the next step is to ask yourself, "What am I really avoiding?" Is it the work itself? Is it the fear that I won't be good enough? Is it the fear of being successful? Understand that it can be more than one of those things or something else entirely.

Acknowledge these fears. You might write them down or even draw them. Next, you might identify some small steps you can take. Action is the antidote to anxiety, so even starting with the smallest action can get you going.

One way to move past the fears is to imagine that you are sitting in front of a closed door. Your new life is on the other side of that door, but you have been unwilling or unable to go through it. Notice what this feels like in your body, mind, and emotions. Try this out. Go up to that door and open it. You don't have to go through it. You can just look through the open doorway. Take your time observing what's on the other side of that door. Then, if you want, you can step into what's on the other side—with the promise that you don't have to stay there. It's just a moment in time to experience what it might be like on the other side. You always can come right back to where you were.

Once you are on the other side of that door, you may find that it's kind of nice there—fun, even. You like it! You might look back to where you had been, which now seems sort of dark and boring. You no longer want to go back there. If so, close that door behind you and enjoy your time in your new, brighter life.

Susan L. Atchison

Belonging

*We are driven by five genetic needs:
survival, love and belonging, power, freedom, and fun.*
— William Glasser —

Personal Reflections

I've never felt like much of a "belonger." In some ways, I did not feel like I belonged to my family. I remember being in my bed at around age 5 and wondering, "What am I doing here?" Have any of you ever felt like the outsider in your family? Or even in the world? Then you know what I mean. And perhaps, because of that (or maybe it's just coincidence), I've never felt particularly comfortable or close to others in groups. Maybe being an introvert as well as a secretive Scorpio has something to do with it. Maybe it was due to underlying depression or anxiety. Maybe it is my past lives influencing this life. Maybe I'm from another star system. Who knows?

People have two main needs: to belong to a group and to shine as an individual. Some of us are better at one than the other. As a counselor, I often hear how people do not feel like they belong. They struggle to feel wanted by, and important to, their family or their friends. This feeling of not belonging is painful to them.

And pain it is. Brain studies have shown that when people feel rejected, their brains register reactions similar to those when they have been physically hurt. We are wired to belong.

Loving Insights

Most beloved souls, belonging is a primal need for humans. Without belonging to someone, an infant would die. Belonging is woven into every fiber of humanity's being. This is the reason you see so many groups—both positive and negative. People have an innate need to belong to something or to be with others.

Belonging is also important in the Heaven world. A soul belongs to a soul group, and when it returns home, that soul is met by their group and joyously welcomed. While the soul may later head out to explore or learn again on its own, it knows at its core that it has a home.

Belonging is expressed on an even higher level by the innate knowing that each soul is an extension of the Creator. Truly, you belong to the Universe. You are part of what makes everything tick. You are part of the ultimate love and source of all life.

Each soul needs to recognize all the ways in which it is part of something larger. Your atoms come from the very stars. You breathe the same air that others do—even those you dislike. Your food is grown from the Earth, and when you consume it, you are partaking of Mother Earth. When you eliminate, it is returned to Mother Earth to be purified and reused. You are a part of the cycle of life in every way. It is time for the souls on Earth to find a new balance between independence and belonging. This is your mission for this lifetime: to balance yourself in these polarities. Find the beauty in each, allow yourself to be part of each, and celebrate each.

Inspired Actions: Tips and Tools for Transformation

Tips

Bring your focus to your life. What did you eat at your last meal? How many people were involved in growing, processing, distributing, and making that meal? Do you see how you are connected to each of them? Give thanks for their dedication and labors.

Reflect on your activities, whether they are raising a family, working, doing physical activity, or self-expressing through something like art or music. How are you connected with others with these things? Many others make it possible for you to do those activities. Did you drive today? Someone provided the vehicle, the roads, the stoplights, the insurance, and the laws designed to keep you safe. All of them are supporting you. Pause for a moment and send out thoughts of appreciation for all these people.

Tools

Sit in meditation and imagine, or see in your mind's eye, the many connections you have to others. You may see them as lines of light going out from you to another to another to another. Then see how these people are connected. The person who supported you by serving you lunch is also supported by their family, friends, teachers, and many more. Envision all those lines of light radiating out.

Now, see how you are connected to and supported by your ancestors—all the people who worked to make their lives, and their children's lives, better. Envision how each of your ancestors was connected and supported in their lives and how those light lines came through your ancestry line all the way to you. All these beautiful light lines come together in a finely woven gossamer net of light that lifts, supports, and protects us.

If you believe in past lives, also see your past lives, and bring light lines to all those who supported you in those lives. Allow those light lines to come expand to those people's descendants and come forward to the current incarnations of all those people.

You are fully connected with the Universe. Feel the Divine Light pouring through your body. Allow yourself to expand and be open to your connection with your soul group on the other side. Feel the peace and harmony of being a part of something so holy. You belong. You truly do.

Betrayal

If you're betrayed, release disappointment at once.
By that way, the bitterness has no time to take root.
— Toba Beta —

Personal Reflections

We often think of betrayal in terms of "big" betrayals, such as adultery, abuse by a teacher or spiritual leader, a sibling stealing an inheritance, or an employee embezzling funds. However, consider some less obvious betrayals, such as a colleague presenting your idea as theirs or someone sharing with others what you told them in confidence. You probably can name some of your own.

Betrayal hurts tremendously because for someone to betray us, we had to have been close to them and given them out trust. It's not really a betrayal if a stranger robs or burglarizes you. It's the close, personal relationship that turns a crime into a betrayal. Betrayal robs us of an attachment, puts us in a bad position, and erodes our sense of trust in ourselves and in the world.

Loving Insights

Ahh, my beloveds, how hurtful the topic of betrayal can be! Who among you has not at some time felt betrayed by those around you? It is the nature of humanity's desires rubbing up against each other.

Betrayal is a loaded word; it is a house of plywood built on a ledge of sand. You only can be betrayed by someone from whom you expected something. But were you really looking at that person? Were you truly seeing them? Did you not see that they are following their own path, however crooked it might seem to you, and that they are actually compelled to do so? Can you see that they are working through their own lifetime of despair, loneliness, grief, greed, and all the other human emotions?

If you did, you would see that they did not, in fact, betray you. What they did was follow the scent of their own trail, much like when a tracking dog has a cloth waved in its face. The dog will take off following the trail with its head down, nearly oblivious to anything else but the scent it is tracking, regardless of where that scent might take it. So, too, does the person who "betrayed" you. Their head is down, and they are following their inner scent. Your expectations are not going to be found on that trail.

Learn to open your eyes and see this truth. Learn to listen to your intuition more carefully. Signs were given, but few were received. This is not your fault, and this is not a criticism. This is an understanding that you have more power than you thought you did. As you become wiser and more connected with your inner guidance, you will be more easily guided toward good choices and helpful people.

Cut the energetic cords that have kept that betrayal "alive" as if it were still happening in the present moment. To keep that betrayal in the forefront of your mind is to be imprisoned by it. The "betrayer" has moved on, but you are stuck in the moment. There is little to nothing you can do other than move on as well.

Inspired Actions: Tips and Tools for Transformation

Tips

I love the book, *The Little Soul and the Sun*. In it, author Neale Donald Walsh tells of a little soul who wants to learn a really big lesson and decides to go to Earth to experience forgiveness. But then this little soul realizes that to have an opportunity to forgive, someone will have to do something bad to it. The little soul despairs, wondering what other soul would take on such an onerous task that would require them to lose touch with their Light? Just then, a soul friend steps up to say, "I will. I'll do that for you." The little soul is moved to tears that another soul would make such a sacrifice.

What if the person who betrayed you is like that friendly soul, taking on the very difficult task to fulfill that role?

Tools

After experiencing betrayal, dedicate yourself to using meditation and affirmations to move yourself back into a healthy, loving, and harmonious way of being. Here are some to start you off:

- "I am free from all past behavior of others that I have found hurtful."
- "I am ready and able to move forward in my life."
- "I accept that this happened and that I did not like it. I now release it and focus my attention on what I wish to bring into my life. I am free."
- "I allow my heart to shake off all hurts and betrayals and to be open to receiving joy."

Create a ritual to neutralize the pain of betrayal:

- Write down what happened, and all your feelings about it, then with the intention to let it go, shred or burn that paper.
- Go out in nature, find a sturdy tree, hug it, and give all your betrayed feelings to it, asking it to return those feelings down to Mother Earth. Remember to thank the tree for this service.

Envision your Higher Self meeting with the other person's Higher Self. Ask what the lesson of this betrayal was. Try to be open to any part that you might have had in it. For instance, did you betray that soul in a past life? Ask both of your Higher Selves to come together to help you bring this experience to a positive completion. This may include you forgiving the other person. You also may ask for forgiveness. Even if you feel you had no part in it, you can ask for forgiveness for carrying around the feelings for so long. Ask that they continue to help you with this until the experience, and the betrayed feelings, are dissolved.

Bitterness

*I loathe my life; I will give free utterance to my complaint;
I will speak in the bitterness of my soul.*
— Job 10:1 —

Personal Reflections

Do you know someone who is bitter about something? You might notice that their bitter attitude affects almost all their other relationships and experiences. They are not much fun to be around. It's as if their mind is stuck on a single track—everything in their lives gets filtered through or comes back around to whatever it is they are bitter about. You can even see it in their expressions and body posture.

The negative impact of bitterness on the person holding onto it is so powerful that the Bible addresses it in many verses. Let's tune in to see if the wisdom Loving Insights has to offer is similar to what the Bible says about bitterness.

Loving Insights

Children, behold the havoc that bitterness can wreak in your life. Bitterness is the hardened encrustation left when resentment is carried a long time and solidifies, much like old food solidifies into a dense mess that is hard to clean off your pots and pans. Similarly, bitterness is challenging to clean off your internal landscape, and the acidity of it will corrode you from the inside out. Be aware that once you start down the path of bitterness, it may be difficult to turn back. Bitterness becomes like the bars of a prison cell that you have built up and placed around yourself. Now you have those bars to be resentful and bitter about as well. Whose responsibility is this? You. You are the one who has the power to remedy this.

What is the antidote for bitterness? To counter bitterness, you must let go of what you thought should have been or should be. This admittedly is not an easy task for everyone; if it were, you would not have found yourself in this bitter prison. However, only you can perform the heroic task. So, consider yourself a superhero—put on your cape and mask, gather your superpowers, and begin to use them to remove the bars of your bitter prison.

Make the decision that you no longer want this. Make the decision that you are willing to move forward in your life to appreciate what is right at this moment and not stay trapped by what you thought should have been or should be.

Bring your focus to one small portion of your life. Do you have enough food to eat? Be grateful. Do you have a part of your body that is not in pain? Be appreciative of that part. Do you have clean air to breathe? Celebrate that you are taking in that breath. In the moment of doing this, allow everything else to fall away and only concentrate on that one part.

In that moment, you will not have resolved your entire life, but you will have found a moment of freedom from your prison. That moment also opens the doorway for your virtuous helpers in spirit to come and assist you; they often cannot reach through the bars of your prison. Help them help you.

Inspired Actions: Tips and Tools for Transformation

Tips

If you could use the powers of a superhero to remove bitterness, what superpower would you use? Would you freeze it? Blast it into outer space? Can you imagine having the ability to dissolve something? Dissolve that bitterness. Maybe your superpower is to turn things into something else. Transform bitterness into beauty. This is like alchemy—transforming lead into gold.

Tools

Don't dwell on your bitterness, how it came to be, or how long you've had it. That keeps you stuck in it. Make the decision that you choose to live differently now. For one of my friends, when old, restrictive thoughts would come up in her mind, she would say, "I remember when I USED to think that." By doing that, she neutralized the thought, put it in the past, and did not condemn herself for having had that thought. This allowed her to immediately return to more productive thinking.

Some people are naturally adept at making changes just by using their mind while others find it more effective to incorporate something on the physical level. If you need something more physical for focus, find a rock. Put your bitterness into that rock (you may want or need to have several rocks for this) then take the rock(s) to a pond, lake, or ocean. Intentionally release your bitterness by throwing the rock(s) into the body of water. You can use your voice as you do this if you want. You might make a clear statement, such as, "I no longer carry this bitterness." The water into which it was thrown will cleanse the bitterness and return the rock to a natural, neutral state.

Alternatively, you can write what you have been feeling bitter about and rip the paper up, run it through a shredder, put it in a fireplace, or bury it in a hole in the ground.

What other ways can you think of to physically remove bitterness from yourself?

Let all bitterness and wrath and anger and clamor and slander be put away from you, along with all malice. Be kind to one another, tenderhearted, forgiving one another, as God in Christ forgave you.
— Ephesians 4:31–32 —

Bliss

*Now may every living thing, young or old, weak or strong,
living near or far, known or unknown,
living or departed or yet unborn... be full of bliss.*
— Dhammapada —

Personal Reflections

Bliss! Isn't that what we all are looking for? But wait—what IS bliss? Is it sitting on the sofa eating bonbons? Is it getting married? Is it birthing a child? Is it finishing a marathon? Is it sitting in Heaven on a cloud all day? How do you do that when you have to go to work, do the laundry, or pick up the kids?

Loving Insights

My beautiful ones, the concept of bliss is a memory from your time in the Heaven world. When there, you truly are in eternal bliss. That does not mean there is not work to do; making yourself or "yoursoul" useful is part and parcel of bliss. Helping other souls is the ultimate bliss. However, in the Heaven world, you are able to accomplish tasks without the interference of the ego, which is a defense system created by a wounded personality that holds back so many people on Earth. Imagine life without conflict created by ego. This is bliss.

It is possible for you to glimpse and even attain bliss on this Earth. Sit quietly. Empty your mind of all your desires, your aspirations, your hopes, and your dreams. These are driving you to find a kind of bliss. Yet all too often when you get there, bliss is fleeting or not really there at all, so you set a course for another destination. What would it be like for you to simply breathe into your heart and know you are indeed a manifestation of the Divine? Feel the Divine breathing with and through you, pulsing in your very veins. You are like a fetus, who is absolutely wanted, cherished, and loved, floating in the womb of your mother and being fed by the umbilical cord that connects you to your source of nourishment. You are in bliss. Allow yourself to exist quietly in this sacred space. Allow your mother to hold you and cherish you. Surrender. This is bliss.

Inspired Actions: Tips and Tools for Transformation

Tips

Could it be this easy? As a counselor—and a person—I have questions about this. Doesn't conflict create growth? But maybe that's only if we have a need for growth. Perhaps in the Heaven world, there is no need for growth, no rough edges of ourselves to smooth out by bumping up against others?

Once we are able to be in bliss, the behaviors of others that previously would have caused conflict do not affect us. We understand that their behaviors are a reflection of who they are and not actually directed at us. Our rough edges have been smoothed, so when we bump into each other, it is gentle rather than harsh.

Tools

Matt Kahn, one of my favorite spiritual teachers, suggests that as you look at—or even think about—others, say to yourself, "May you be blessed." Being kind, helping others, and the act of giving all stimulate our brains to produce the neurochemicals dopamine, oxytocin, and serotonin—also known as the "Happiness Trifecta." When you make this a habit, you may find yourself feeling happy more often. As happiness becomes your natural state, you may begin to live in bliss.

Here is a full blessing from me for you:

> May you know the Light
> May you be the Light
> May you share the Light
> May you be blessed.
>
> May your loved ones know the Light
> May your loved ones be the Light
> May your loved ones share the Light
> May your loved ones be blessed.
>
> May all beings know the Light
> May all beings be the Light
> May all beings share the Light
> May all beings be blessed.

May you be blessed—may you be blissed!

Susan Atchison

Compassion

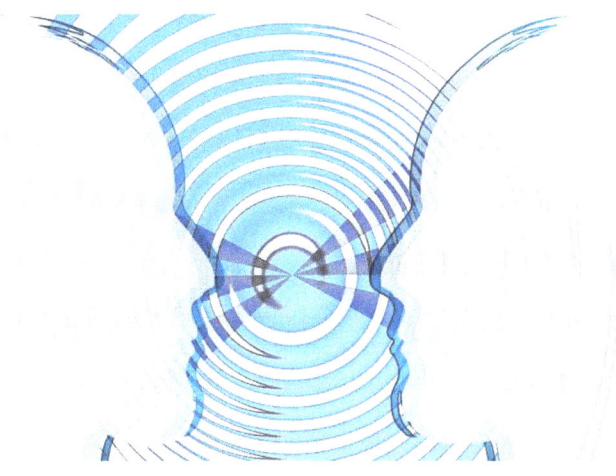

*More smiling, less worrying. More compassion, less judgment.
More blessed, less stressed. More love, less hate.*
— Roy T. Bennett —

Personal Reflections

Compassion seems like a great idea. Certainly, the world could use a little more of it. But sometimes compassion can be a double-edged sword. Too much compassion can get us into trouble, like when we overlook behaviors or problems that could then hurt us or others. Compassion also can wear us out. When I searched online for a quote on compassion, the first entries that came up were regarding compassion fatigue. That's when you get drained by understanding and giving—and giving and understanding. It is a real challenge for therapists or parents, teachers, and friends. Why is it that compassion, which seems like such a great idea and quality, also can cause so many problems? Is there a right amount of compassion? How do we know what that might be, and how can we navigate it?

"Navigate" may be the perfect word. You can see that the word "compassion" starts with the word "compass." Is this because it is pointing us in the right direction for our lives? But compassion also contains the word "passion," so compassion calls us to go in the right direction with the appropriate energy.

Loving Insights

My child, compassion is at the heart of every spiritual teaching in your world. Some teachings have forgotten this—or have covered it in rules and judgments—but compassion remains the elixir of Light. Compassion is your heart opening to receive and pass on the great wisdom from Above. Your brains are wired to release feel-good chemicals when you allow this heavenly compassion to pour through you.

When you feel compassion, you are moved to think differently about someone or something. This does not always mean that you need to act differently. Remember that people can feel your energies, and the energies you send out into the world circulate around and affect what is happening. So perhaps you might envision your compassion as a means for lifting the energy around a person or situation so their own creativity and connection with their inner guides can come through. This allows that person to become more wise and self-empowered and make a difference in their own life. Here you have a win-win. It is not overwhelming or tiring for anyone to continually send out compassionate thoughts; it's the misuse of action that has been tiring you.

Inspired Actions: Tips and Tools for Transformation

Tips

Help yourself learn when an action is needed and when it is more empowering for the other person to create their own solutions. This does not mean that you need to stay distant or emotionally detached from them, but rather that you adopt the Buddhist concept of "detached compassion." Bhante Sujatha, a Buddhist monk, has said that you can imagine yourself and another person as though you each were in a small boat. If the other person is upset, you can pull your boat over next to them to comfort them. However, if you pull them into your own boat (if you take their upset onto yourself), you'll both go down.

Tools

My personal beloved teacher, Billie Topa Tate, a native Mescalero Apache healer, offers a beautiful and simple spiritual practice that can be done anytime and anywhere. When you see, read, or hear about a person who is feeling distressed, you can silently (or out loud) state, "Whatever virtuous energy this person needs, let it be so now." If you are in a place to do so, you can hold your hand out and imagine the energy flowing to them. In this way, you are opening the door for the higher beings of Light, who know more and are more advanced than us, to bring healing to the person.

The Buddhists are well known for their Loving Kindness meditation, which consists of mentally sending positive energy (prayer) toward others. One example might be:

> May you be happy.
> May you be well.
> May you be at peace.
> May you be free.

You also can set your own internal signal as to when you should step forward to help with action and when you should give the person space to resolve their own difficulties. Sit quietly and ask for a body signal to be given to you. It may be that if you are to take an action, your body will lean forward, and if you are to hold the space while the other person takes their own action, your body will stay still. Or you may find that your index finger buzzes or lifts up for actions, and your pinkie finger buzzes or lifts up to indicate that you should not take action at this time. Signals can come in any form and are individual to you.

Compassion arises easily when we are in the gamma brainwave state, which unifies all our senses and allows us to feel the Oneness of all that is. Gamma brainwaves can be enhanced by meditation, and the Loving Kindness meditation is ideal for this. You also can listen to binaural music to activate gamma brainwaves. Taking these steps to nurture our compassion helps us connect with the Light within us and to feel our connection with the Source of all Light.

Criticism

*Any fool can criticize, complain, and condemn—and most fools do.
But it takes character and self-control
to be understanding and forgiving.*
— Dale Carnegie —

Personal Reflections

Being criticized stings! We say that criticism is "given," which implies that it could be a gift, but it really does not feel like one. When critical words are said by a key person at a key time, those words can lodge inside you like a burr. You may even come to believe the criticism, and it can burn holes in your self-confidence. I still remember some of the criticisms I received. If they happened a long time ago, I may not remember the exact words, but I remember the feeling.

Loving Insights

Cherished ones, criticism is used by people when they are feeling uncertain and wish to protect themselves. "The best defense is a good offense," has been said. If you were to look deep into the heart of people who tend to criticize, you would see a mess that is dark, spiky, inflamed… you get the picture. These people have been the recipients of criticism themselves. Their brains have learned to think along those lines, and their hearts have not yet awakened to the truth that everyone is simply doing the best they can.

Let us pause for a moment and distinguish criticism from helpful guidance. What is the difference? Guidance is when a path has been clearly laid, such as when engineers precisely plan the trajectory of a rocket. If something goes off course, steps need to be taken to bring that projectile back into alignment on the planned path. Criticism is often aimed more at the individual than at the behaviors. It is a "one-up" ploy designed to help the criticizer feel superior to—and thus protected from—the receiver.

While it can feel hurtful to be on the receiving end of criticism, learning to take it with a grain of salt will let you maintain a peaceful mind. Examine what is offered to determine if there is any truth in it or anything you can learn from it. Even a pile of chaff might have one grain of wheat in it. Then recognize the rest for what it is: the criticizer trying to lighten their own inflamed load by tossing flaming sticks out at you. If you feel called to do so, you can offer a prayer or invocation that healing be brought to this individual, or you can simply build your energetic wall more securely around you so these flaming branches will bounce off.

Inspired Actions: Tips and Tools for Transformation

Tips

Sometimes in my adult life, because of my having felt criticized as a child, I have reactively felt criticized by someone when that was not their intent at all. Awareness is the key here. Notice whether there is a pattern either in what someone else says or in your reactions to what they say. It is very helpful to learn to separate what is yours from what is not yours.

I like the idea of distinguishing criticism from helpful guidance. Criticism often feels as though it is coming AT you. Guidance is more of a gentle hand on your arm to encourage you to change direction a little bit. For instance, when a ship sails, it does not go directly from Point A to Point B. Rather it tacks from side to side. If the ship is sailing north, it will sail a little bit northeast then a little bit northwest yet all the while ultimately still going to its northerly destination.

Tools

When you are criticized, or when you are hurting from the memory of having been criticized, reclaim your power with these affirmations:

> I am my own self.
> I listen for the intention more than the content.
> I trust my inner guidance.
> I know when to listen and when to walk away.
> I am a good person.
> I am growing in a healthy, balanced way.
> I know my own truth, and it sets me free.
> I allow the Divine to guide my choices.

Following is a fun and energizing exercise to get the sting of criticism out of yourself. You'll need a bare wall and two or three pillows (using pillows of different sizes and weights can be helpful). Facing the bare wall, pick up the pillow you feel best represents the impact of the criticism on which you are focusing. Imagine putting the criticism into that pillow. Now envision that the person who criticized you is standing in front of the wall. Toss the pillow of criticism to that envisioned person. As you toss it, use your voice to make strong statements (out loud), such as:

> "I give this criticism back to you!"
> "This is your criticism, not mine. Take it back!"
> "I don't want your criticism!"

Keep picking up the pillows, putting a criticism into them, and throwing them back while using your voice to talk to the person who criticized you until you feel cleansed. Once you are free of the criticism, put something positive into the energetic space you just cleared. You can imagine filling the space with violet, gold, or white light or infusing it with healthy self-confidence, self-image, spontaneity, or whatever feels right to you.

Criticism, and how you receive it, may inform your life and relationships in some small way, but it doesn't ever have to ruin your life or relationships. Remember who is giving the criticism and joyfully separate the wheat from the chaff. AKA throw pillows!

Depression

There are wounds that never show on the body that are deeper and more hurtful than anything that bleeds.
— Laurell K. Hamilton —

Personal Reflections

When I first drafted this section on depression, I was thinking I had been spared from depression in my life. But I was wrong.

Now I am certain that my father suffered from undiagnosed and untreated depression. His father had been an alcoholic who often left the family without money. Family lore says there was one time when my father had nothing to eat for three days. His own resulting depression manifested in anger and withdrawal. Early in my life, when I was quite little, he would spank me for… who knows what? How much trouble can a little girl get into? (I saved most of that trouble for my teenage years….) I think he just needed to get some anger out. He would come home, eat dinner, yell at my sister and me, then get up from the table without a word and go to his bedroom where he would stay the rest of the evening. One of the results was that I entered my adult years expecting men to be angry with, and then withdraw from, me.

Perhaps as a result, for years I endured what is called "Persistent Depressive Disorder." Someone with this condition may have low self-esteem and a general feeling of inadequacy and have an overall gloomy outlook. For me, it manifested in a nearly complete lack of joy in my life. When you are immersed in something, you don't always realize what is happening; it's just your normal. I finally became aware in my 30s that something might be amiss when I would drive down the street in my beautiful neighborhood, pass by neighbors, and feel completely unable to smile at them. I didn't know how to smile at them.

Persistent Depressive Disorder is like living in a gray cloud. In contrast, clinical depression is like a big wet blanket over the soul; it affects everything in someone's life. Any type of depression often is a hidden illness because we can't necessarily see it when we look at someone.

Loving Insights

Most beloved children, understand that you are honored for your journey on this Earth. Indeed, your world is a difficult one to live in at times There are so many challenges for its inhabitants. Depression is a modern world illness. It comes from not getting enough sunlight and oxygen, from a lack of healthy minerals in the soil, and from toxins and viruses that never were present in earlier times. People are facing many challenges within their bodies.

But it is not just the body that is being challenged. It is the mind and the soul. People are separated by technology even though they may believe it is connecting them. They are not looking people in the eyes, and the eyes are the gateway to the soul. We need to look at each other to have a soul-to-soul connection. Today there is a deep longing for something that people do not know how to fill. The lack grows on itself, and depression sets in. There is not one cause, so there is not one solution.

A depressed person should be honored for the battle they are facing. Give them time to slog through the difficulties. Providing simple support can do a world of good for them. If you are the one who is feeling depressed, set your goal that this will pass. Be gentle with yourself while at the same time being firm. Get out in the sunshine as much as possible. Do whatever you can to take in more oxygen—even simple, easy exercise is helpful. Getting out and about can be healing.

On a spiritual level, depression often is a dampening down of creativity and the expression of true self. Who are you meant to be? Expression of your true self is most easily found when you are open to your Source connection. This allows the energy of the Creator to flow through you.

Find a way to sit and focus on that stream of Light coming from the Heavens above and flowing into the crown of your head. Allow it to pour through you. Envision it lifting up and washing away the dust, dirt, and grime of depression. Then let it bring in new ideas, new inspiration, new activities, and new love. Do this every day, even if it is only for a few minutes or just one minute. Just do it. Set this as your goal; it can be done.

As you continue to do this, you may feel a lightening of your mood, a shifting of the energies. Can something so simple make such a change? Yes, indeed, it can. While it may feel like you are not in charge of your life when you are in a depressed state of mind, the few moments you sit in contemplation of the Light ARE within your control. Focus on those few moments and watch your life slowly change. Even if nothing else seems like it is within your control, these few moments are. So, sit down and say, "I am the captain of my own ship," then envision that Light pouring through you. Do it again. And again. And again. You might be surprised at what will begin to unfold.

Inspired Actions: Tips and Tools for Transformation

Tips

If you are feeling depressed, know that it is not your fault. While there are steps you can take to work your way out of it, you did not call this onto yourself for some obscure reason, and you are not being punished for anything. It just is.

Tools

I like the idea of getting a full nutritional workup. Sometimes our emotions are thrown out of whack because we are not getting—or not absorbing—the nutrients we need. In my 20s, I became aware that I have gluten sensitivity along with some allergies. For instance, if I ate rye, my palms would itch and I would become (even more) emotionally irritated. It's important to know whether your body is reacting to what you put in it and is stressing your system on top of the emotional challenges of what you have lived through or are living with.

If you have the resources, the Pfeiffer Medical Center (www.hriptc.org/index.php) specializes in the assessment and management of biochemical imbalances. You can see a local naturopath who can help you determine what might need balancing in your body. At a more budget-friendly level, one of my current favorite nutritional guides is Anthony William, the "Medical Medium," who gives easy yet helpful detoxing plans in his books. Please see the Resources section to find more about his work.

Once you have addressed any physical imbalances, you may find it helpful to talk with a therapist. Therapists are trained to help you find resources, both internal and external. If needed, a good psychiatrist can help to find the right medication for you.

Exercise also has been found to be of great help for those struggling with depression. I know, I know—when you're depressed, it's much harder to get off the couch. When I was at my lowest point, I would drag myself to the gym by telling myself that I only needed to walk around the track once or twice. It was a big little lie! Once I started moving, it was easier to walk a bit farther than planned or even to jog a little.

As the Loving Insights section mentioned, getting out in the Sun can be helpful. Taking a "forest bath," where you spend time in the forest under the trees, has been found by many to be soothing and renewing. "Grounding," where you put your bare feet on the ground, is said to discharge negative energy from your feet into the soil and then recharge you with positive energies from the Earth.

Depression also partly can be a result of suppressing a creative impulse. In what ways would you be creative if you could be? Is it jewelry making, painting, drawing, sewing, designing, composing? There are infinite ways to be creative. Can you take one little step, such as coloring in preprinted adult coloring books or stringing some beads together to make a bracelet?

Drumming can be an expressive activity that links creativity with physicality. Find a drum—it can be anything from a Native American drum, bongos, or even an upside-down pot. Begin to create a rhythm with your hands, with a drumstick on your drum, or a wooden spoon on your pot. If you want, you can begin by drumming along with a song that has an easy and compelling beat. You may find that you start to move your body or chant or sing with the rhythm. Some people like to make statements along with the drumbeats.

Examples might be:

Beat	**Beat**	**Beat**	**Beat**	**Beat**	**Beat**	**Beat**	**Beat**	**Beat**
I	claim	my	power!	De	pres	sion	be	gone!

One of my clients had amazing improvement simply by using a technique, taught by Matt Kahn, that involves praising yourself for everything. I call it, "Praise Without Ceasing." The way he says to do it is to praise yourself for even the simplest of actions. Did you go get something out of the refrigerator? "I am the BEST refrigerator door opener ever!" Did you walk the dog? "No one walks the dog like me!" Like many of the other techniques, this helps rewire your neural pathways by resetting them from negative to positive.

Taking these small, seemingly insignificant steps can help because even a little step begins to reestablish the flow of energies in our lives.

Most of all, be kind to yourself. As noted, depression can be the result of multiple causalities. When you are depressed, that's when it can be the hardest to reach out for help or to keep trying things until you find what is helpful for you. To support yourself, try to picture the future you who is healed and reaching back through time and space to you, encouraging you to keep going. May you find what you need to become the best you that you can be.

Despair

Life begins on the other side of despair.
— Jean-Paul Sartre —

Personal Reflections

The American Heritage® Dictionary of the English Language, 4th Edition, tells us that "despair" is both a verb (to lose all hope; to be overcome by a sense of futility or defeat) and a noun (complete loss of hope).

Yikes. Hope is what keeps us going in hard times, isn't it? Without hope, we stop looking for solutions because we think there are none. From there, I imagine it is quite easy to sink lower and lower, to feel darker and darker, to fall into despair.

I can only think of a couple of times when I've felt despair. I recall, decades ago, lying on top of my bed and crying and begging for whatever or whoever to please help me. But I didn't even really know what was wrong. I only knew that I felt desperately unhappy. I didn't know why and, for sure, did not know what to do about it.

Loving Insights

Despair is when you sink into yourself and lose contact with your ever-present Source. Despair truly is disconnection from knowing that all is one and all is well. You are focusing on your outside conditions and your inside emotions about those conditions, but you are not seeing the golden threads woven in and through every aspect of the tapestry of your life.

Were you to be still, you might focus on these threads until you perceive them in whatever way is natural to you. Ask your golden threads to connect you to what it is you wish to resolve. Are you experiencing a lack of love? Find the golden thread that leads you to love. Focus on that golden thread and begin to use it to connect yourself to love. Are you in dire financial straits? Likewise, you can find a thread that will lead you to financial stability.

First, you must believe you can do this. Begin by practicing it. Sit quietly and begin to imagine your threads. If you cannot imagine them, try this: imagine that you can imagine them. As you focus on your golden threads, you may find a moment or two of peace, which then can lead to another moment or two. These tiny moments are like a trail of breadcrumbs you can follow, nourishing yourself along the way until you reach your goal.

Inspired Actions: Tips and Tools for Transformation

Tips

The time that I felt the most in despair (when I collapsed on my bed and cried out, "I need help! I need help! Help me!"), I wish that I could tell you that the skies opened and I saw angels who came down and gave me what I needed. But that didn't happen. Instead, I wore myself out and went to sleep. Somehow, though, things started to get better. Sometimes when we are forced to our knees, we have no option other than to surrender. It cracks open our shell so we can receive what is needed, which often is NOT what we thought we needed.

Once I was going through a rough time with a client who always seemed to need more than I knew how to give. I felt stuck in unknowing, and when I am feeling stuck, my mind tends to circle around and around the issue or the problem. That doesn't help me come up with a solution.

I sat down to meditate and clear my mind. That's when a phrase came into my mind: "There is always a solution." The beauty of this is that when you say it, whether out loud or to yourself, it takes your mind off the problem, at least for that moment. Your mind can pretty much only think one thought at a time, so saying this gives your mind a mini break from the problem. Once I started saying, "There is always a solution," my mind started to look for that solution instead of dwelling on the problem. That's when unexpected ideas would pop in—and voilà!—I'd have a solution. That can begin your move out of despair.

Tools

When I am stuck with an issue, or I'm helping work through an issue with a client who feels very stuck, it is helpful to look for options. When you focus on and talk about the options, it moves the attention and the energy from the problem to the solutions.

Brainstorming often is used to come up with problem-solving options. To do this, you take an issue and come up with ideas about how to address it. No idea is too outlandish; none are to be judged or criticized. The principle is that even a completely undoable idea (such as, "Let's ship our garbage to the moon") may spark another idea that is more actionable. You may begin to see patterns in the ideas.

You can try this, too. Take a piece of paper and write an issue in the center then start writing down any and all ideas about what you can do about it. You might put the more "out there" ideas farther away from the center and the more doable ones closer to the center. You can even color-code them if you want. Feel free to put this exercise down and pick it up again later. Maybe you only can do a little at a time. That's okay. Good ideas often need a spark and then time to quietly grow and develop, much like a seed needs quiet time underground to germinate. As best as you can, trust the process.

Remember, a few moments of thinking about options or the smallest action can be the beginning of your journey out of despair.

Determination

*It will never rain roses;
when we want to have more roses,
we must plant more roses.*
— George Eliot —

Personal Reflections

If you've ever listened to or read motivational talks or books, you'll likely get the concept that determination is a good thing. A great thing! Be determined to be a success and keep going. Just do it!

That is good advice because who among us can't use a little help staying the course? It's normal and part of the journey to encounter difficulties, which can be either external roadblocks or internal barriers. That's one of the reasons we have 12-step programs, MasterMind groups, life coaches, and the like. They help keep us determined to succeed.

But what about the other side of determination? Sometimes we can get something in our minds and become determined to make it happen when it's not a good thing at all. Think about a stalker. He or she is determined to make the object of their affections love them. Clearly, that's an extreme example of determination gone wrong. But if you look carefully, you might find a time in your life when you were determined to be, do, or get something that maybe wasn't best for the good of all. I know I have.

So, how do we utilize determination in our lives?

Loving Insights

Divine ones, determination is setting a focus for the flow of energy. There is not a right or a wrong flow of energy. It is just energy. What is right or wrong is the intention and reason you are flowing that energy. A healthy flow of energy is when you are using it to lift up yourself and others. A bonus is when you are intentionally including the increase of light and love in the world. The determination to achieve this goal will attract much help from the other side because the increase of light and love is a worthy intention. You can envision that the flow of energy goes out like a beautiful fountain. The sight and sound of the flowing waters is enchanting and beneficial to all who see it. The waters then return to the source, bringing with them the benefit of the oxygen they have absorbed while splashing through the air.

On the other hand, determination that exclusively serves your own ends can be envisioned like a dark vacuum hose; its purpose is to suck up things and bring them back to the user. This can be done individually or in groups or even masses. Think of genocide in which people attempt to extinguish whole populations so they, themselves, can have more of whatever it is they want.

Thankfully, most determinations are not that extreme, so how can you determine the expansive versus contractive uses of determination? This is simple. Just remember the words "expansive" and "contractive." When you are determining to do something, does your heart open? Is your breath deep and full? Does it bring a smile to your face? Does it bring beauty into your life? Then it is expansive determination. If it feels like you are leading with your chin or your head, if you are scowling or gritting your teeth, or if you are feeling fear, anger, jealousy, or any of the lower vibration emotions, then it is contractive determination and will require a great deal more of your own energy to move toward the end point.

Inspired Actions: Tips and Tools for Transformation

Tips

What is it you are determined to do? How will you feel when you have achieved it? What will it do for the people around you? Once you have determined (Ha! no pun intended) that your path is an expansive one, how can you keep a healthy, balanced level of determination?

Energy is like water. Water flows. Water finds its way around obstacles. If you are on a path of expansive determination, envision the energy flowing like water ahead of you. When you come up against obstacles—because most worthy journeys will have obstacles—know that the water can and will find a way around them.

Tools

When you have a healthy determination to accomplish or manifest something, you can use the themes given in mythological journeys to help you. Joseph Campbell has written a beautiful synopsis of these themes in

The Hero's Journey. In most heroes' journeys, the story begins with the hero living in a community yet somehow not feeling content there or as though they fit in or feel at home. The hero may feel a strong pull to embark on an unknown quest, or they may be prompted to begin their journey when they meet someone or discover something, such as an item with magical properties. On the journey, the hero faces great challenges that often are overcome through ingenuity and sometimes with the help of others. After overcoming adversity, the hero is rewarded with special powers or a magical gift. The hero then returns home and uses those new powers or gifts for the benefit of their community. This is in alignment with the message from Loving Insights—that determination is best used for the betterment of all.

Even if you don't think you have magical powers or helpful friends, you can take your own hero's journey. Envision the path along your journey and just see, sense, or know the points along the way that seem to be challenges or obstacles. You might envision an obstacle in a symbolic way. For instance, if a person is standing in your way, you might see them as a boulder. See yourself as water flowing over or around that boulder, dissolving the boulder, or even floating the boulder away. If the obstacle is a lack of something, such as finances or education, you might see this as a dry spot in the river. How will this be remedied? You might see the skies opening up and rain coming down or a spring coming forth from underneath the ground or even people bringing water to fill that spot.

You don't have to know where or how, in real life, these things will happen; you are using the powerful symbolic language of your subconscious to rewrite the scene. Once you have envisioned it in symbols, your subconscious will understand that the obstacle has been overcome and will help bring this about in your life.

Disappointment

*When you find your path, you must not be afraid.
You need to have sufficient courage to make mistakes.
Disappointment, defeat, and despair are the tools
God uses to show us the way.*
— Paulo Coelho —

Personal Reflections

Disappointment can be a real downer. Who among us has not looked forward to something and then had it either not happen or not go as expected? It's disappointing!

As I thought about disappointment, it occurred to me that it may come from having expectations. We expect something to be a certain way because we feel it will make us happy. Then the outcome is not the way we expected, and so we feel disappointed—NOT happy.

Is the issue having expectations though? Aren't we supposed to have some expectations? We get married and expect to be happy. What's wrong with that? Doesn't that help set the tone and intention toward having a happy marriage? We expect to get a promotion, a raise, or a new job. Isn't that setting our intentions for the positive outcome? But if it doesn't happen, we are disappointed and not happy.

Loving Insights

Beloved of beloved, your human world is based on what you perceive to be reality. In this reality, you prefer to have events happen in a logical, linear fashion (such as education, job, marriage, children, promotion(s), retirement). However, your universe is not actually a logical one—at least not in the way you think about logic. Rather, it is logical in the sense that people and events are connected by energy streamers. Many of these streamers were set up before you ever arrived on this planet in a physical form. Let's say that you set up a streamer to learn a lesson about forgiveness. Logically, you would follow the energy streamer along the path that will lead you to this lesson, which is more valuable to your soul than any other experience you could conceive.

In such a case, perhaps you followed along the path laid out by your society. You completed your education, you secured a job, and you got married. The next step in your logical sequence would be a promotion, but your coworker steps in front of you, maybe doing something you would view as unethical, and grabs the promotion you thought would be yours. Disappointing, is it not?

Actually it's not—if you are looking at the situation from a greater perspective. What do you have to learn from this? Perhaps it is the aforementioned forgiveness. Perhaps you are meant to be somewhere else, doing something else, and this situation was designed to help get you there. One great disappointment can lead to internal reflection, and internal reflection can lead to new awareness, which opens new doors to new experiences in your life.

So, is it really disappointing? As you move along the path of spiritual development, you may still feel disappointment, but that is likely to be transformed quicker and quicker. You wanted something and even deserved it then it didn't happen. Whereas before you were greatly disappointed and dealt with that emotion for months, now you already are looking for the lesson or the opportunity in that situation because what you really were looking for was happiness. This answers the question of setting expectations. You are looking for happiness. Expect happiness. Look for it everywhere, and it will happen for you. There is no disappointment in that!

Inspired Actions: Tips and Tools for Transformation

Tips

Understanding situations as lessons can be very helpful. When you are feeling disappointed, you can ask yourself, "What am I learning here?" Maybe it is to be patient. Maybe it is to be more loving, to go back to school, or to be open to a new opportunity that you would not have considered before.

Let's take a closer look at the word "disappointment." It can be broken into "dis" and "appointment." The dictionary definition of "dis" is "apart, asunder, away, utterly, or having a privative, negative, or reversing force." You had an "appointment" with someone or something, and that got negated or utterly (torn) apart. Therefore, your expectations were reversed.

Tools

If you are feeling disappointed, reflect on how you had expected to feel if what you'd wanted to happen did indeed happen. Now bring that feeling into your life—either in reality or in your imagination. Your brain cannot tell the difference between feelings created from reality or from imagination.

Once you have reflected on what it is you had expected to feel should the experience have happened as desired, there is another effective way to bring that feeling into your life. Help someone else feel that way. Here are some examples. If you had wanted to buy a special house, and it fell through, join Habitat for Humanity and help build a home for someone in need. If you had hoped for a promotion and did not get it, begin to mentor someone at work or volunteer at a community career center.

When you help someone else achieve similar goals, you will find that you feel as happy as you would have if you had you gotten what you thought you wanted. Plus, you will make connections that may help you achieve your dreams, too.

Then you are no longer disappointed—you are appointed!

Empathy

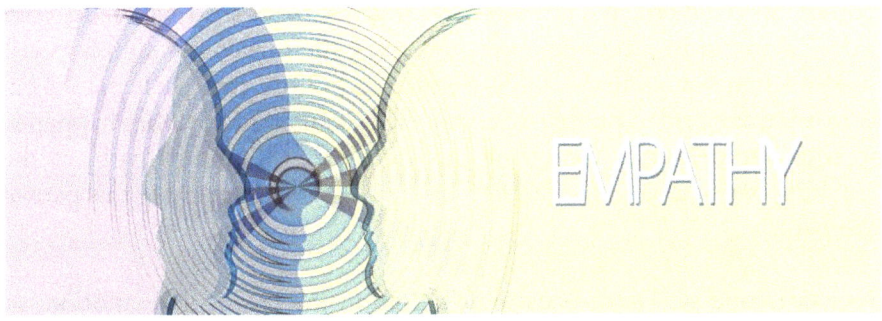

*Too often we underestimate the power of a touch,
a smile, a kind word,
a listening ear, an honest compliment, or the smallest act of caring,
all of which have the potential to turn a life around.*
— Leo F. Buscaglia —

Personal Reflections

Empathy seems like one of the highest vibration emotional states. It is a wonderful gift to have and share.

Most of us probably know the difference between empathy and sympathy, but just in case it is new to you, here is a short synopsis of how to think of them. Sympathy is "I am sorry this happened to you" (sometimes with "you poor thing" either verbally or nonverbally attached to it). Empathy is "I understand what you must be feeling and may even feel your pain." You might imagine that one feels better than the other to the recipient.

Loving Insights

Holy ones, the quality of empathy was placed in human hearts so you truly could begin to understand the difficult journeys many people are traversing. Sympathy creates a kind of a divide, saying, "You are over there having this problem, and I am, in a sense, almost looking down on you for having this problem." Empathy, on the other hand, says, "I am with you in this problem. We can walk this journey together. I will be by your side." Many times, the person experiencing the difficulties simply needs to know that someone else understands and honors their challenges. That is worth the world to people who may feel ashamed of what has happened to them or may feel like others are victimizing them. Empathy is the reaching out of a hand for them to hold and guide them along this part of the path.

Not everyone on Earth is naturally gifted in the use of this emotion, so there will be times when people seem incapable of offering true empathy. This is okay because people are just who they are, no more and no less. Accept what is given, forgive what is not given, and keep moving forward in your own life.

Inspired Actions: Tips and Tools for Transformation

Tips

Just as professional athletes practice the basics over and over regardless of how talented they are, so too can we revisit some basic principles around offering empathy to another.

Many trauma survivors have been the recipients of a lot of unsolicited "spiritual advice," suggestions for how to think about what just happened to them, or stories about how the other person had something similar happen to them. These often are not helpful at this early stage because, during trauma, the cognitive function of the brain turns off. The survivor basically is a walking wound. Even if it is done with the best of intentions, addressing a survivor like this is similar to poking your finger into a physical wound; it not only does not help the wound heal, but it can reactivate the pain. In doing these things, we are coming AT the survivor rather than creating a soft, safe space for the survivor to rest in so they can begin to heal.

Tools

Here is an example of empathy in action. Ask the person, "What is it like to be you right now?" Then just listen. Don't interpret, don't try to make it better, don't placate or judge them or share your own experience. Just listen and acknowledge. You might ask, "What do you most need to hear right now?" Then say their answer back to them. Of course, this only works if it is done with sincerity.

Matt Kahn suggests that the only way to respond to someone who has just experienced trauma is saying what you would say to a small child: "I am so sorry this happened to you."

When we have been hurt, we naturally are wired to reach out to others, so, if appropriate, a touch on the hand or the arm or a safe hug can be helpful. Remember that it needs to be what feels comfortable to that person—let them set the tone for touch.

Brené Brown has a wonderful, short, animated video about the difference between empathy and sympathy in which she says, "Empathy fuels connection; sympathy drives disconnection."

Another helpful resource is the book *The 12 Stages of Healing: A Network Approach to Wholeness* by Donald M. Epstein. He outlines the stages of healing, taking them from Stage 1: Suffering, in which the person is feeling that "Right now, I am helpless. Nothing works at this time," to Stage 12: Community, in which the person has made it through the healing journey and wants to share "the wisdom and understanding gained through our healing journey."

For more information on either of these helpful tools, see the Resources section of this book.

Susan L. Atchison

Emptiness

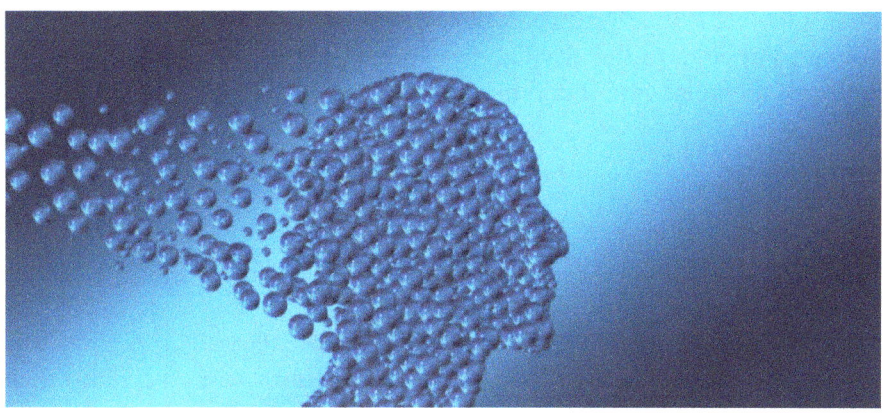

*Emptiness, which is conceptually liable
to be mistaken for sheer nothingness,
is in fact the reservoir of infinite possibilities.*
— D. T. Suzuki —

Personal Reflections

Here's an interesting question: If Buddhism teaches us to empty our minds and be unattached, then why are so many people unhappy because they feel empty or unattached to someone?

Perhaps this is the distinction. An empty mind is one that is not filled with anxious thoughts about the future or guilty, angry, or ashamed thoughts about the past. An overall empty feeling is felt more in the body or soul. People feel empty when they have lost someone or something that was meaningful to them or have lost sight of their meaning and purpose in life.

For example, my friend Jan had a difficult time finding her way. As a young woman, she trudged through a series of unrewarding jobs, none of which lasted very long. Inside, though, she was nurturing a secret. She wanted to be a massage therapist. During Jan's formative years, she had not had anyone encourage her to share her hopes and dreams—in fact, quite the opposite—so Jan had not shared her secret hope with anyone. Finally, though, she told a colleague at work. The very next day, that colleague left a flyer on her desk with an ad for a massage school. Jan followed up and, to this day decades later, she is a dedicated and talented massage therapist. She found her life's purpose.

Loving Insights

It is a common human condition to want to feel attached, important, and purposeful. Souls become incarnate here on Earth to move along their journey, to gain experience, and to learn lessons. Emptiness can happen when a soul has stalled out on its journey. When this happens, a person can have a beautiful life, which, from the outside looks as if they have everything—a good job, family, home—yet inside, this person is not feeling it. He or she feels empty. That is because they are no longer developing in the most important way.

Emptiness comes from a lack of passion and purpose. This person has not found their calling or has strayed from it. They may be successful, or they may just be going through the motions. They need to get back in touch with their inner connection with Spirit, known by whatever name they feel comfortable using. When you breathe into your heart, you will feel the embers of passion begin to stir again. Allow yourself to be guided to each next small step that will open the gates to more and more passion and purpose. You know you can do this. Allow your mind to complain or argue then, as if you were helping a toddler, take it by the hand and turn it in the desired direction.

Inspired Actions: Tips and Tools for Transformation

Tips

Be open to wherever guidance might come from; it could be coming from someone or something you never expected.

Emotions: Emptiness

There is an interesting story about a traveler who, when walking down a street, comes across three men working with bricks. One man appears to be tired and somewhat sullen, a second is neither unhappy nor happy, and the third seems energetic and happy. The traveler asks what they are doing. The sullen man complains, "We are in the hot Sun laying bricks all day long." The neutral man replies, "I am building a wall." The happy man smiles and says, "I am creating a beautiful church where people can come together, worship God, and find fellowship." When you have purpose, that purpose can fill the even small, mundane actions so they no longer feel empty.

Tools

What is the opposite of emptiness? This might be different for each person, and for one person, it may be different from moment to moment. The opposite of emptiness might be fulfillment, happiness, or love. Once you have decided, for the moment at least, what the opposite of emptiness is for you, try this exercise.

Stand in a place with plenty of room. Imagine there are five large circles on the floor in a line (one right next to the other as in the diagram). Each circle is big enough for you to stand in and even move a bit within.

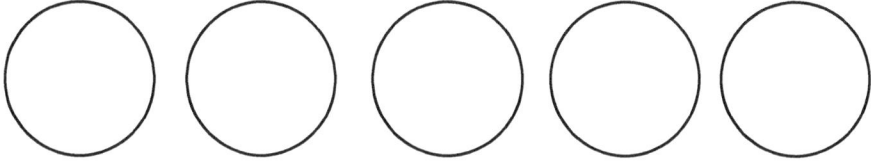

EMPTINESS   **PURPOSE**

The first circle holds or represents the state of Emptiness. The fifth circle is whatever you named as the opposite of Emptiness. For the sake of this exercise, let's call it Purpose. Each circle between Emptiness and Purpose is a step on the way from Emptiness to Purpose.

Now, stand in the first circle, Emptiness. While you are standing in this circle, let your body demonstrate what it does when you feel empty. Your shoulders may droop. Your face may fall. Feel the feelings of emptiness. BE Emptiness.

Next, you have a choice. Some people like to jump over to the fifth circle right away. In this circle, you are Purpose. Your body stands as it would when you are filled with Purpose—most likely tall and energetic. Your face smiles. By jumping to the fifth circle, you get a taste of what that state of being would feel like. Another choice is to steadily progress from the first circle to the second and so on to the fifth without first jumping to get a taste of Circle 5.

If you chose to jump to Purpose, return to stand again in Emptiness. Usually, after feeling Purpose, you won't want to stay in Emptiness very long! Next, step over to the second circle. This is a bit better than Emptiness but not yet filled with Purpose. Let your body and emotions feel what this is like for you. Then move to the third circle—this one is in the middle, so you will feel half Emptiness and half Purpose. Now step to the fourth circle. You're almost there, so you probably feel yourself shaking off Emptiness and beginning to fill with Purpose. Now return to the fifth circle and soak in the entirety of Purpose. Stay here as long as you'd like. Internalize it. This is the true you.

Faith

*To have faith is to trust yourself to the water.
When you swim, you don't grab hold of the water
because if you do you will sink and drown.
Instead, you relax and float.*
— Alan W. Watts —

Personal Reflections

"Have faith" people tell us—often when it is the most difficult time of all for us to "have faith." Those in the Christian faith are given the story of Job, from whom everything was taken and who still had faith, or of Abraham, who was asked to sacrifice his son and was prepared to do so. These kind of seem like extreme cases, don't they? How many of us could have such faith? It seems like a tall order and a lot to live up to.

Other religions also address faith. The Hindu spiritual practices give us lots of mantras, the chanting of which is said to bring about positive change. Is there faith involved in that, or do the mantras just sort of work mechanically on their own, like sending "bots" out into the Universe?

There are different kinds of faith. Are we talking about "situational" faith—faith that something will happen—as in faith that we will get the job? Is it the larger kind of faith—faith in God? Or are they really one and the same?

Honestly, faith has been a challenge for me. I just haven't felt as though I had the faith that I see in others. Maybe that's been part of my spiritual search. On my third trip to a silent meditation retreat led by Amma Karunamayi in India, I finally cried, but not from having found a deep connection. I cried because I just couldn't find the deep devotion in me that I witnessed in so many people around me. Despite this, there's something inside me that keeps bringing me back to faith. It just seems to be easier to see it in others than in myself.

I am told that, after she died, Mother Teresa's journals revealed that she had her own faith challenges. (Who knew, right?) Now, I'm no Mother Theresa, but one of the purposes of having great spiritual leaders and teachers is to show us qualities to emulate. So maybe, like her, if I just keep on keeping on, faith will keep growing.

Loving Insights

Many blessings to you, my precious and holy children. Know that faith of the heart is the essence of all true growth. As you awaken in your innermost recesses, you begin to become aware of a pull to be with certain people, to read passages and books, or to pray, chant, meditate, sing, paint, and dance. Faith is the unseen current that pulls you toward your destination. Faith is also the chasm that looms large before you. Faith is both the question and the answer.

Faith can be your Achilles heel. Do you know what that means? It means that it can be the one weakness that could bring you down. Why is that? It is because faith is a journey, not a destination. Faith is the name of all the stops on the train tracks.

Think about the movie *Forrest Gump* in which the main character says, "Stupid is as stupid does." Well, faith is as faith does. Faith sitting on the shelf just gets dusty. Faith must be dusted off, featured prominently, and shared. This does not mean pushing any particular brand of religion or doctrine on someone. Rather, it means holding the positive expectation that all will be well. For indeed, all is well.

Inspired Actions: Tips and Tools for Transformation

Tips

Think back in your life to a time when you had a positive expectation that became a reality. Sometimes, in the rush of life, we focus on all the things we need to do or want to have (thus also focusing on the lack of those things). We forget about the times we were given what we needed. That's why a little reminder can be helpful. Faith is like a muscle that gets stronger as you use and stretch it.

Try reading inspiring stories and books. *Ask and It Is Given* is an excellent one.

Spiritual groups, such as gatherings at churches or temples, can provide support for faith in God. For faith in everyday life, you might form a support group to help each other stay focused on that faith.

Tools

Every night before you go to sleep, treat yourself to a prayer or invocation to strengthen your faith. An acronym poem creative exercise can be helpful. For this, you write down vertically the word, symbol, experience, or situation you are considering. Doing this moves us out of the logical left brain to allow for more creativity. Then start each line of the poem with a word that begins with the first letter on that line. Often it seems that the words written down naturally will progress from the challenge to the solution; however, it may not. Let your writing be just what it is.

Following are two examples using the word DOUBT:

Doubt seems to dog me.
Out of the blue, it takes hold,
Undermining my faith.
But then I remember that I can
Trust my heart to guide me right.

Don't you know that it's not okay?
Other people just don't seem to
Understand what I'm going through.
Because of that, it's up to me to
Transform and transcend.

Following are a few examples using the word FAITH:

From the beginning
And now again and again
I focus my attention
To my Creator, who
Helps me always.

Facing
Adversity
I
Thank
Him

Freeing myself from
Absence of faith
Intentionally
Turning my attention to
How to surrender

Remember, faith is both the question and the answer.

Fear

*Fear is not of the present, but only of the past and future—
which does not exist.*
— A Course in Miracles —

Personal Reflections

I was facilitating a practice hypnotherapy session with my colleague, Pat. She wanted to work on how she felt a bit afraid of almost everything—from physical activities like walking down the street to more internal activities like feeling confident about speaking up. She had a powerful session. At the end of it, she said, "You know, I just realized that I always think of what could go wrong, but I never think of what could go right."

This statement had a profound effect on me. At that time, I had been practicing out of my home and was considering moving my business into an office. I had a lot of fears about that. What if it didn't work out?

When Pat made her statement, it stopped me in my tracks. I thought, I know what could go wrong if I do rent an office. I could be responsible for a year's rent. But I had NO idea what could go right—the possibilities were infinite! Well, you probably can guess the rest of this story. Thanks to Pat, I did move into an office and began to enjoy those infinite positive possibilities.

Loving Insights

Beloved children, when you look closely at most human emotions, fear is at the root of them. Anger is fear. Rage is fear. Jealousy is fear. Greed is fear. And so on. Fear is the great net that captures all else. Fear is the great human challenge as well as the great human lesson.

When you conquer fear, you will have conquered most of life. Your life will open in ways you never imagined. Fear holds you back, and faith moves you forward.

Begin now by identifying fear where fear is present in your life. Some areas may be obvious while others may be much more subtle. When you find fear, acknowledge it. Fear began as a tool to help keep you safe, but then it ran amok. Admit the fear then ask that it be lifted from you. Here is a helpful prayer for you:

> Heavenly Father, Creator of All That Is—I ask you now to reach deep into the depth of my being and neutralize all fear tendrils, all energy created by, or connected to, fear. Neutralize it and lift it out to be transformed into positive energy for the Universe. Help me feel that transformation in a very real way. Breathe your breath of life into me now so every aspect of my being is filled with Your faith. I ask that this be done now, and so it is. In full faith, Amen.

Inspired Actions: Tips and Tools for Transformation

Tips

If you are afraid to do something, ask yourself what is behind that fear. One way is to simply sit quietly and notice your breath as you internally ask each question. Typically, a deep, full breath with a complete exhalation (expansion) indicates truth while a short, shallow breath (contraction) is a clue that there is an untruth.

Some questions you might ask include the following:

- Is this a fear to keep me healthy and safe in a positive way (like fear of swimming with sharks)?

- Is this my fear or someone else's? Sometimes we take in the fears of our parents. Science has shown that we actually can hold fear in the genes we have inherited from our ancestors, even from several generations back.

- Is this fear based on a false belief? An example would be a fear of speaking because you think everyone in the audience will laugh at you.

If the fear belongs to someone else or is from a false belief, the prayer given in Loving Insights would be useful.

Tools

You also can identify where in your body you are experiencing the fear and breathe beautiful colored light into that area. Allow the light to diffuse the fear until it no longer exists. You will feel a wonderful, new freedom as you do so. God already forgives you for your secret fears, debts, trespasses, mistakes, and sins. Can you do the same for yourself and others?

One of my favorite prayers is a particular version of the Lord's prayer. Did you know that the Lord's prayer has several variations? Here's a brief tour through some of them.

I was raised Protestant, and we used this first version:

> *And forgive us our debts,*
> *as we forgive our debtors*
> (Protestant)

Then I married a Catholic, and so I learned this version:

> *Forgive us our trespasses,*
> *as we forgive those who trespass against us*
> (Matthean version used by the Roman Catholic Church)

In researching for this book, I found this version from a different translation of the original Aramaic:

> *Loosen the cords of mistakes binding us,*
> *as we release the strands we hold of others' guilt*
> (from https://njlc-fh.org/aramaic-lords-prayer)

A few years ago, I attended a workshop by a man who channels Yeshua (Jesus), and he used this Aramaic translation:

> *We know that You already forgive us our secret fears,*
> *As we choose to forgive the secret fears of others*

I like this last translation most because it helps me understand how many times we misbehave (whether you label it "debts," "trespasses," "mistakes," or "sins") because of our inner fears. This helps me not judge others but to choose to forgive. That is woven through this entire book.

Forgiveness

*The truth is, unless you let go, unless you forgive yourself,
unless you forgive the situation, unless you realize that
the situation is over, you cannot move forward.*
— Steve Maraboli —

Personal Reflections

Do you know anyone who is having trouble forgiving someone in their life? For some people, their hurt feelings interfere with every aspect of their life. Thoughts of what happened seem to intrude even when they are out at a social event. This person may find it hard to forgive because it might feel like they are condoning the hurtful action done by the other person. Sometimes people go right up to the doorway of forgiveness and even look through, but just can't quite seem to step over that threshold. Not forgiving can seem like it gives us control or power while forgiving feels like we are giving up the power to condemn the other. Actually, it is the opposite.

Loving Insights

Beautiful beings of Light, the sound of the word "forgiveness" is a clue to the true meaning of it. "For" "give" "ness"—it is to give, to give what perhaps is not deserved yet, and to give it anyway. Until you forgive, you are trapped in your own stew of emotions. It has been said many times that forgiving is done for yourself and not for the other(s). That is true. Indeed, it is for yourself, but it is done for the other as well.

The poison of the vitriol directed at another person is sent into the energy field and is held there until it is neutralized or dissipated. Therefore, when you forgive, you are neutralizing the energy you sent out in the past. Forgiving works to cleanse you. It also is for the good of the one whom you felt did you wrong, AND it is for the good of humanity.

Every act of forgiveness lightens the load on the Earth's energetic field. When you forgive, you are doing your part to aid help lift the vibrations of humanity. Moreover, each time you forgive, you make the next time easier. You are less trapped by the poisonous emotions that are part and parcel of unforgiveness. You are free.

Inspired Actions: Tips and Tools for Transformation

Tips

Being in a state of unforgiveness takes a real toll on our bodies. It keeps us in a state of anger, resentment, and bitterness—all of which signal to our bodies that we are not safe. Our bodies then prepare to fight or flee by releasing adrenaline, shortening our breaths, and decreasing digestion.

Remember the quote, "Living well is the best revenge"? That's because when you choose to live well, you are giving your body the gift of a healthy, relaxed state of being.

What if forgiving does not seem warranted? I am reminded of the story of a family who lived in France hundreds of years ago during the time of absolute power by the monarchy. The son in this family broke a law, got arrested, and then was scheduled to be executed. His mother went to the king and asked for mercy. The king replied that the son clearly had done the misdeed and did not deserve mercy, to which the mother replied, "Yes, he did it. And the punishment is just, but that is not mercy. I am asking for mercy." The king got her message and commuted the boy's sentence.

Tools

Can you imagine that there could be a time—even way, way far in the future—when you found a way to forgive? Sit quietly and let yourself be in that time. See, hear, sense, and feel yourself. What does it feel like in your body, mind, and spirit to have forgiven?

Then, in your mind, come back through the years. Let's say that you are 40 now and you imagined being 90 and having forgiven. Come back to age 80. Had you forgiven by that point? Are you glad you forgave? If yes, come back again, to age 70, and ask yourself the same question. Keep coming back until you find the point in time at which you feel you made that step into forgiveness. It may be closer than you think. Pause there and notice what factors helped you step over the threshold to forgiveness.

If you were not able to imagine reaching the state of forgiveness, yet you still are hopeful for relief, find someone who you see as having been able to forgive another. You do not need to know this person personally; he or she could be a person you read about or saw on TV. Allow yourself to become this person for a few moments. Feel what it is like for that person to live in a state of having forgiven.

If you need to, and it seems helpful to you, you can ask for the presence of a spiritual master, such as Jesus, Buddha, or Quan Yin, to come and help you. Once you have experienced what it might be like to have forgiven, come back to the present. Are you willing to start this journey in real life? Reclaim yourself and live well!

Susan L. Atchison

Fulfillment

*Occasionally in life there are those moments of
unutterable fulfillment, which cannot be
completely explained by those symbols called words.
Their meanings can only be articulated by the
inaudible language of the heart.*
— Martin Luther King, Jr. —

Personal Reflections

What is fulfillment? I love this quote by Martin Luther King, Jr., that says it is a feeling in the "inaudible language of the heart." When we feel fulfilled, don't we often use the expression that our "heart is full" or even "overflowing"?

What fulfills me is very different from what fulfills you—and every other person on Earth. That's what makes us so wonderfully diverse! There are some common denominators, such as love of family and friends. Then there are the many variants, such as work, hobbies, creativity, and so on. Fulfillment can change, too, can't it? What may have felt fulfilling at one time can later feel stultifying.

Loving Insights

Sweet ones, your heart is the center of your universe. It is your lodestone and your guide star. Within your heart is all you need to be fulfilled. Your mind is sometimes connected with your heart, and sometimes your mind is trying to supersede your heart or divert it to another route entirely.

Listen to your heart—always listen to your heart—for it will guide you unfailingly in the right direction for you at the time. Your heart is not the same in any two moments yet it flows along nevertheless. The air you breathe, the nutrients you eat, the quality of the water you drink, and the nature of your thoughts—all of these are flowing through your bloodstream as an unending passage of influences. Your heart's environment is ever changing. What does not change are the goals for which you came to Earth. Within your heart is the calling that brought you here. It is in following this calling that your heart will feel complete or what you call "fulfilled." Another way to say it is that your heart is filled full.

While the expression of that calling may change from time to time, the inner calling does not. A calling to uplift people may be expressed in art, in providing medical services, in singing, in counseling, in spiritual practices, in teaching, and more. You are fulfilled when you are uplifting people, regardless of which of these avenues you are enjoying at the moment.

So, listen to your heart, listen to your heart, and listen to your heart. It will always guide you truly.

Inspired Actions: Tips and Tools for Transformation

Tips

Sometimes life seems so chaotic, and we have so much input coming from different directions that it can be difficult to listen to our heart. Sometimes our mind jumps into the action to tell us what the mind thinks we should be doing or should fulfill us. At these times, the simple act of taking a deep and full breath with a complete exhale can slow us down so we are able to focus on our heart.

Tools

Find yourself a quiet space and take out pen and paper. Write down all the times you were doing something when the time just flew by. It doesn't have to be an income-producing activity! That's a fallacy our culture likes to focus on. You might have been playing with the kids, volunteering at a cat shelter, or organizing your closet. Write as many of these times down as you can remember. The writing doesn't have to be linear; you might put circles all around the page(s). Put this aside overnight; the next day, you may have discovered some more.

Once you feel your list is complete, look for the common thread in these instances. If you don't see one at first, ask for it be shown to you. You might take colored pens or pencils and draw connecting lines between entries. You might find yourself drawing pictures or having beautiful insights. Now you have discovered the inner essence of what fulfills you!

Susan L. Atchison

Gratitude

*I am grateful for what I am and have. My thanksgiving is perpetual.
It is surprising how contented one can be with nothing definite—
only a sense of existence.*
— Henry David Thoreau —

Personal Reflections

So much has been written about the importance of being grateful or having gratitude. Some authors have taken it a step further, saying that we should not be "grateful" because that implies an underlying lack (like being grateful because someone let you in out of the rain). Rather, they say, we should express appreciation. I like to keep it simple and say what I am thankful for.

A few years ago, my car set my house on fire, and we lost virtually everything. While we had great insurance and were able to move into a luxurious rental home while we were rebuilding, I still felt traumatized. So, I began to say, "Thank you." I didn't always mean it fully, but I kept doing it. An easy time to do it was when I was at the end of a long day of working and rebuilding. I would walk up the stairs to my bedroom on the second floor, and with each stair step I would say, "Thank you." Usually, I was so worn out that I couldn't even think what I could be thankful for, so I would just say, "Thank you." Then I began to do that with each step on the way back down in the morning. Ultimately, these thank yous took the place in my brain that otherwise might have been occupied with stress, worry, or self-pity. Now, when I look back on that time, I remember the thank yous rather than the stress. I am thankful that I did that exercise.

However, sometimes the focus on appreciation and gratitude almost can be used as a cudgel on ourselves as well as others. I call that New Age bullying. I see this regularly in my office. Clients will come in with some difficulty, explain it to me, then tell me that they don't know why this is bothering them because they have a nice house, good spouse, plenty of food, and so on. Essentially, they are now suffering twice—once with the issue that caused them to come see me and a second time by lecturing themselves that they should Just Be Grateful.

Loving Insights

Child, you must know there is no appreciative difference between expressing gratitude and expressing appreciation. Both are uplifting emotions coming from the heart and rising to the Heaven world. Both open the door so there can be a two-way channel between the receiver on Earth and the givers in Heaven. The wording is just a construct by people; the important aspect is the feeling and vibration. So, feel appreciative or feel grateful; express either and you will experience the same results. The goal is to train your mind to pay attention to the blessings in life.

The human brain is wired to look for danger or for circumstances that feel unsafe, so it can take charge and correct that situation. This is all well and good, and certainly was needed for survival; however, you now are living in much different times, for the most part, and your well-being can be more easily achieved through sustained application of energy principles.

Lifting your consciousness through gratitude is one of those principles. Pause for a moment and reflect on how you feel when you think about a difficult situation or a worry. Then reflect on how you feel when you think an appreciative or grateful thought—no matter how "small." It might be simply that you woke up today or that the Sun is shining or that most of your body feels pretty good. That's the feeling you want to have, and you are in complete control of it. How do you want to feel in life? Find the smallest way in which you can feel this and focus on that. Breathe into it as if it were an ember and allow it to grow. Continue to do this, and soon you will find that your life is even more blessed.

Inspired Actions: Tips and Tools for Transformation

Tips

Sometimes it seems hard to keep focused on the positive aspects of life. When we get distracted by worries and problems, this alone creates new challenges. When my clients come in blaming themselves because while they are experiencing an overwhelming life difficulty, they haven't been able to stay fully positive. In doing so, they are exacerbating their difficulties by blaming themselves for "negative" thoughts or emotions. I like to say, "That's just called being human." Because we are human, most of us are not perfect; most of us just need to keep stepping up to bat over and over. For me, it's a balance. Acknowledge the "not good," address and process it, then return to a better feeling state. If we try to push down or cover over the "not good," it will fester internally. It's better to air it out in the sunlight.

Once you have done that, you may find it helpful to follow the advice given by one of my early yoga teachers, who used to say, "The mind is like a child; when it misbehaves, you don't smack it around—you take it by the hand and lovingly direct it in the way you want it to go." I love this! The part of our minds that worries and blames and so forth truly is the younger part of us—the part that did not feel in control because it wasn't! But now we are grown, and our consciousness has grown. So, let's just gently take our mind by the hand and guide it to where we would like it to be—appreciative, grateful, thankful, or whatever works for you in the moment.

> *If the only prayer you ever say in your entire life is thank you,*
> *it will be enough.*
> — Meister Eckhart —

Tools

Some people like to keep themselves focused in one of these fun ways:

- Put a "gratitude jar" on your counter. Every day, write on a slip of paper at least one thing for which you are grateful and put it in the jar.

- Make a pact with your friends to share the things for which you are grateful. I've created a game called WRUG4? which stands for "What Are You Grateful For?" You also can use WAUTF? ("What Are You Thankful For?") or any other acronym variation. Text that acronym to your friends at random times, and they agree to text back what they are feeling grateful for at that moment.

- Set a timer on your phone to go off each day. When it does, pause and think of some things for which you are grateful.

You can create your own fun ways to keep yourself feeling grateful.

Greed

Greed is not a financial issue. It's a heart issue.
— Andy Stanley —

Personal Reflections

Greed is one of the seven deadly sins. So, it must be pretty bad.

I'd like to think that I don't have greed. Who wants to end up in one of Dante's circles of the Inferno? Not me! Still, I have been known to worry about having enough… of anything—money, clothes, food, time, you name it. Is that greed? I sure hope not!

Maybe I'm defining it for my own benefit, but I'd like to think that greed is more than just worrying about having enough. Greed is like an addiction. Certainly, someone who wants more and more alcohol or drugs would be said to have an addiction. But we also can be addicted to sex, to work, to food, to anything. We are greedy for things we think will make us feel better. Many of the things about which we can become greedy are good, or even necessary, in appropriate amounts. The nature of addictions, though, is that we naturally develop a tolerance for whatever fuels our addiction. That's when the amount or level of what used to satisfy us no longer does and we need more and more to generate the same level of excitement or satisfaction. The problem comes when the amount needed balloons to excessive amounts and/or interferes with other aspects of our lives.

Loving Insights

Most beloved, the "sin" of greed is not so much in the doing of it as in what causes (or underlies) it—the feeling of being separated from God.

Greed is a person's belief that they do not have enough and will never have enough. It is a hole in the individual's soul out of which good things fall. There is no way to fill this hole because it is created by the separation of that individual from God. It is as if the cord between the two got pulled out and left a gaping hole. The person tries to fill it with whatever most easily captures their attention. For some it is money, for others sex, still for others it may be food. None of this is what they really desire. God does not get angry, nor does God dismiss any soul. God wishes only for that person to return home to their rightful place within the All. But that person moves farther and farther away as they attempt to use their own energy force to please themselves. This is the Big Mistake, what you might call a "sin." Sin is separation; separation is sin. Do not be mistaken that this is a judgment; it is an omission more than anything.

Inspired Actions: Tips and Tools for Transformation

Tips

If greed is the faulty thought that you always need more or that what you have is never enough, then it is based on fear. It is the fear of not having enough—of whatever—to be okay or to feel okay. In a sense, that person's heart is closed, unable to receive or accept what God wants to give them.

So, is the remedy for greed faith and trust? It sounds like all we need to do is turn our attention from lack to connection, from fear to comfort and safety. I guess, like many things, we just need to start from where we are and, little by little, keep focusing on where we want to be. If greed is based on separation, then we would need to connect to release it. One first step is to determine where or with whom we need to connect. Family? Friends? Purpose?

Not feeling like we ever have enough is said to be an issue connected to the root chakra. For those new to chakras, the word means "wheels," and they are like spinning vortices. I think of them like transformers because they take the powerful Universal energy and tamp it down so we can safely take it in. We have seven main chakras that are aligned along our spine, from the top of the head to the base of the tailbone. Each chakra is connected with specific qualities or functions as well as a developmental stage (the emotional needs we progress through as we grow from infancy to adulthood). The root chakra is our connection to the Earth and our feeling of belonging and having enough. Its developmental stage is that of the infant; it is life and death for infants to be, and feel, wanted; to know that they belong to their family, tribe, community; and that there is enough—love, food, time, attention—for them.

When a chakra is out of balance, the qualities it represents will be out of balance in your life. If the root chakra is out of balance, the person will not feel like there is enough. Does that sound like the "root" cause of greed?

Tools

One easy way to bring chakras back into balance is to use crystals. Crystals have "structured" energy—the energy within them is set into patterns of alignment by their physical and mineral qualities. Thus, they can help bring our energies into a similar alignment and allow us to feel more balanced.

To bring greed into balance, you might utilize the services of crystals, such as the following:

- **Hematite** is grounding and calming; it helps you to feel connected to the Earth and supports healthy thought patterns.
- **Smoky Quartz** aids in letting go of the past; it helps clear away what no longer serves you.
- **Black Tourmaline** helps ground you, protect from negative energies, and neutralize anxiety.

How can you use your crystal(s)? One way is to place them at or near the foot of your bed or on the floor by your desk. They will help draw your negative energy back into the Earth while replenishing you with positive, grounded energy.

Another way is to meditate while holding one. Before meditating, be prepared to ask some questions; if you want, you can ask your crystal to help give you answers. What questions can you ask? One approach is to ask questions similar to those advised to people who are challenged by eating addictions. Specifically, before they eat, it is suggested that they pause and ask the "HALT" questions: "Am I Hungry? Angry? Lonely? Tired?" What if we did this each time a greedy thought came up? We can ask, "What is it that I really want? How will getting this thing or experience make me feel better? How long will that feeling last? What could I do instead that would provide more comfort and safety than this thing?"

Have a pen and paper nearby and write down what comes to you. You may find it very enlightening.

Grief

Only people who are capable of loving strongly can also suffer great sorrow, but this same necessity of loving serves to counteract their grief and heals them.
— Leo Tolstoy —

Personal Reflections

I have a friend whose beloved mother passed away, leaving my friend distraught. Even though my friend and her mother were steeped in spiritual practices that teach that the soul is eternal and simply moves on to another dimension after the body's death, that doesn't help my friend when she wants to see her mother's smile, hear her voice, or feel her touch. This devastating loss even ripped away some of my friend's spiritual beliefs; she no longer knows whether she believes what she used to. She has lost not just her mother but also her faith. The void is great, and her anguish is deep.

To say that "it is better to have loved and lost than not to have loved at all" does not help when someone is grieving a devastating loss. It is not our place to tell someone how or when to grieve. It doesn't help that the American society tends to want us to process our grief quietly and get over it quickly. My friend feels not only the loss of her mother and her faith but also the loss of her friends. She has noticed that few can be present with her deep grief, so her feeling of loss is compounded.

While we tend to think of grief as coming from the loss of a loved one, there are other kinds of grief as well. There is the grief of losing a dream (such as not getting a job, scholarship, or relationship for which you had hoped or of having a marriage fall apart). There is the grief of having someone you love become sick. There is the "leaving without goodbye" grief of having a loved one's mind lost to Alzheimer's or dementia. You probably can add several of your own definitions or experiences of grief to these.

Loving Insights

Beautiful children, your time on this Earth plane is limited by design and, for many, the transition to the true life is a mystery. For those who do not have a faith, the loss of a loved one can be devastating because it is as if that person has simply vanished.

For those who are grounded in a spiritual tradition and faith, it still can be difficult because humans are made to interact through their voices, their eyes, and their touch. Losing the physical presence of a loved one cuts deeply and can feel as if part of them was ripped out. The part that is gone cannot be replaced by anyone else on Earth. It is the smile, the laugh, the twinkle in the eye, the voice on the phone, and the gentle touch that is gone.

And yet, your world was designed to be a revolving door. Your time here is precious, and your time in the Heaven world is unlimited. You have chosen to be here on this learning plane for a finite time so you get something you can get nowhere else. That something is the understanding of the importance of connection, and connection is the key to life. When you are connected, everything else begins to fall into place. When you are not connected, you feel truly alone in more ways than one. Your connection to others in this world is a mirror of your connection with All That Is. It is a taste of what is to come. Losing that connection can feel as if you have lost your link with your Source, with life itself.

And yet you have not. Your connection to Source is within you, always present and always accessible. While the amount of comfort needed to restore the feeling of connection to Source—that most secure of attachments—will vary from person to person, the process of reestablishing the connection nearly always will give some solace to the soul.

Inspired Actions: Tips and Tools for Transformation

Tips

You are an individual, and the way you express grief, as well as the way and the time you need to adapt to your changed life, will be individual. Be sure to honor your grief—it is an expression of the love or dreams you had.

Sometimes people who are grieving try to hold it in, fearing that if they really feel it, they will fall apart. However, the opposite is true. Intentionally letting it out is like opening a valve on an overfull container—it releases the pressure and prevents a collapse.

Tools

Create a safe space and time in which you can fully grieve. Set a timer. For that amount of allotted time, really let go and grieve. Curl up into a ball, cry, sob, howl, beat your fists on the bed—let it all out. When the timer goes off, bring this process to a gentle close for now. You can return to it whenever you want.

Journaling can be very helpful while you are in the process of grieving. Writing down your feelings can help you work them out (sometimes feelings seem so confusing that you are not sure what they are) and express them. Journaling also will give you a context later. Often when we look back at a difficult time we went through, we have forgotten some of the nuances of influences that came into play. Having all your feelings and experiences—both positive and negative—written down can help you understand who you were and all the aspects of what you were going through at the time.

Many people find it helpful to connect with a group of people who are in a similar situation because they better understand what you are feeling and thus can support you more than others can. This is why some communities have support groups.

If you cannot find a church or community group, you can look online. Facebook has both closed and secret* groups for people who are grieving. You also may benefit from a therapist who specializes in grief counseling and can help you navigate your way on this unfamiliar and unwanted journey.

> *A secret Facebook group is one that you cannot find by searching; you must be invited to join. The only people who can see the group and its members are the people added to the group. To the public, secret groups are invisible.

Guilt

*There are two kinds of guilt:
the kind that drowns you until you're useless
and the kind that fires your soul to purpose.*
— Sabaa Tahir —

Personal Reflections

Sometimes I feel like I have been the Queen of Guilt. Surely one person could not have been that responsible for doing or saying so many wrong things. What was it that drove me to ruminate every night on all my "wrongs"? I once read that this is a hallmark of an introvert. That was me—the introvert who replayed every conversation to analyze how I could have said something better or whether the way I said it might have offended someone. And those were just the minor transgressions. Lord knows, I've had bigger ones, too—ones that people other than just me might say, "Yes, you SHOULD feel guilty about that!" Is that you, too? Let's see what we can learn about guilt to lift these burdens.

Loving Insights

Beloved one, there is no need on this planet for guilt. As the character of Yoda has said, "Do or do not." What is done is done. Your time is much better invested in making this moment count. Do not waste your precious moments by ruminating over what has happened in the past. If you have truly done something inappropriate—something that you would not do today with today's level of consciousness—then make amends. But remember that having had that experience is likely the only way you know today not to do that thing again. Thus, bless that experience, and bless the You that you were at the time who unknowingly sacrificed her or himself to gain that lesson. Then be as kind to yourself as you would be to others who have made mistakes. Life is about making mistakes; it is not about living perfectly. What would be the point of that? You might as well have stayed in the Heaven world.

Remember also to free yourself from judging those around you. As you judge, so you will be judged—and likely by yourself whether you know it or not.

Guilt is the past. What is your future? Put your eyes on your future and determine to live the best life you can. Perhaps you would like to ask for help from Above. Maybe one reason you erred was that you were not connected at that moment with your guides, your conscience, your Higher Self, or your Creator. Maybe your mistake was a living reminder of that disconnection. So, every day, remember to ask for that guidance and protection.

Inspired Actions: Tips and Tools for Transformation

Tips

One of my teachers, Ann Ree Colton (founder of a religion called Niscience, which means "Knowing"), said that guilt is self-centeredness. It took me a while to understand this because if it was self-centeredness, here was another thing of which I was guilty! But now I am coming to understand that if I am holding onto guilt, I am not freeing up thoughts, time, and energy for the people and experiences around me now.

Tools

Ann Ree Colton gave us an exercise* in which you imagine a two-sided coin. One side is colored silver and the other gold. The silver side has the negative thought on it—in this case guilt. The gold side has the positive thought on it—in this case appreciation. If you feel guilt, imagine that you see the word "guilt" on the silver side of the coin. Then intentionally turn the coin over so you now see the gold side, labeled "appreciation." Do this as often as you need throughout each day. Over time, both sides of the coin will become gold. You will no longer feel the guilt, just the appreciation.

Notice that in this exercise you are not dwelling on or even rationalizing the negative thought. You simply are turning the coin over to see the positive thought. Modern brain research tells us that what you are doing is creating new neural pathways. When you have a thought, it stimulates certain neurons. A chain of neurons stimulated over and over creates a kind of pathway. When water goes down the same path over and over, it will carve a very deep channel—even the Grand Canyon. Thoughts are like that, too. It might not be easy at first to change a thought. Just like gravity naturally would direct a drop of water to the lowest level, a thought tends to want to go into the most deeply carved pathway. But when you stop using a channel, it will, over time, fill up with dust, dirt, or debris that make it harder for anything to flow down into it. If, at the same time, you are creating a new channel and painstakingly using it over and over, this inevitably will become the default. It's science!

*See the Recommended Resources section for a list of the Ann Ree Colton's negative/positive pairings.

Susan L. Atchison

Hopelessness

*One should... be able to see things as hopeless
and yet be determined to make them otherwise.*
— F. Scott Fitzgerald —

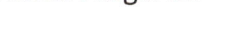

Personal Reflections

Hope is the spark that keeps us going. No matter how bad things seem, if there is any amount of hope for the situation to change, we can bear it. Once hope is gone, once someone is hopeless, there seems to be no way out. This must be one of the most difficult situations to live through. Some people, though, have told me that it was when they hit their lowest point and fell to their knees (some figuratively and some literally), crying out, "Help me!" that they made a spiritual breakthrough. The Light broke through, and they were given hope.

Loving Insights

Blessed children, hope is the thread that connects you to the Divine. When one has lost sight of that thread, the lack of it is what makes this person feel separated. Like a baby separated from her mother, she does not know what to do or how to fix it. She just cries and cries until she has worn herself out.

The truth is that the Divine connection is never truly lost or disconnected. It is only the person's perception that it has been lost. Sometimes the darkness has covered it until the person cannot find a way to grasp it again. Sometimes the person has their back turned to it. They are looking in the wrong direction. You may have had this experience in your physical life—you have misplaced something and are looking everywhere except where you left it. Do not judge the person who is feeling hopeless. They just forgot where they left their hope.

Instead, bring compassion and joy. Yes, joy. While they are unable to perceive that they could feel it, they need to know that joy is out there and it is available for them to have again. What used to bring this person joy? What used to create a spark in their life? It doesn't have to be something big; in fact, often it can be seen as more realistic to choose a smaller spark. Breathe on that spark gently; ask the person to help you breathe on it. Together, you slowly can bring it back to life again. This is how you remedy hopelessness.

Inspired Actions: Tips and Tools for Transformation

Tips

Whether it is in you or someone you know, you can begin right now to instill a small sense of hope. First, listen. Really listen—even if it is to yourself. Honor that person's journey. Many people simply don't feel listened to. I'm not saying that this is the cause of hopelessness, but it doesn't help. Don't try to fix it or deny it or argue with it. Just listen to it.

Tools

Find an activity that interests you. It might be something as small as liking (or that you used to like) to take a walk. Now put one foot in front of the other. You don't have to go very far. You know what they say: "The longest journey begins with the first step."

Take it "slow by slow." Slowness is rather undervalued in our American culture. But someone stuck in hopelessness is likely temporarily incapable of doing much more. Just take a baby step for now.

As we have discussed in other sections, the brain needs to be rewired. Like with meditation, consistency is more important than quantity. A little bit every day wins over a lot once in a while. You are laying down new neural pathways.

An effective way to lay down new neural pathways is an easy Kundalini yoga practice, which incorporates a simple chant or "mantra" (a tool for the mind) with a "mudra" (a motion or dance of the hands).

A chanting mantra calms your mind, and the mudra soothes your nervous system. This practice is said to improve sleep, boost energy levels, refresh your brain's neurotransmitters, and reset neural patterns so you can create a more fulfilling life.

When using the mantra in the meditation, you have the option to repeat the words any of these three ways:

1. Singing (or saying out loud)—The vibrations of the spoken words correspond with outer actions.

2. Whispered—The vibrations of the whispered words correspond with your mind.

3. Silently (saying the words mentally only)—The vibrations of the silent words correspond with your spiritual self.

Complete mantra (language: Sanskrit):

Sa Ta Na Ma   Ra Ma Da Sa   Sa Say So Hung

(Pronunciation: Sah Tah Nah Maa   Rah Maa Dah Sah   Sah Say So Hung)

Each word in this mantra has an individual meaning; the whole of the mantra honors the totality of life, from the creation of life through birth on to death and including the transformation of consciousness, resurrection, and rebirth, which allows us to consciously experience merging with the infinite and oneness with God.

Posture: Sit in easy pose, with your chin level and slightly tucked back, or sit on a comfortable chair with your feet flat on the floor. Whichever way you sit, try to keep your spine straight.

Eyes: Your eyes are open only a tiny slit. Focus on the point between the eyebrows.

Mudra: Place the wrists over the knees. As much as possible, keep your arms and elbows straight.

Chant the **Mantra:** *Sa-Ta-Na-Ma Ra-Ma-Da-Sa Sa-Say-So-Hung* in a rhythmic way as you press the tip of the thumb to the tip of each finger sequentially with each syllable. Do this with both hands at the same time. For example, it would be:

- Sa—Tip of the thumb to the tip of forefinger on the same hand
- Ta—Tip of the thumb to the tip of middle finger on the same hand
- Na—Tip of the thumb to the tip of ring finger on the same hand
- Ma—Tip of the thumb to the tip of pinkie finger on the same hand

Then start over with the thumb to the forefinger for "Ra Ma Da Sa" and again for "Sa Say So Hung."

Continue these cycles for 3–11 minutes. When your chosen time is complete, inhale deeply through your nose. Hold the breath as you stretch your arms up into the air and then lower them in a sweeping motion. Stretch and move the head, torso, arms, hands, back, belly, and as many of your muscles as you can up, down, and around.

Once you have moved and stretched, bring your hands to your heart center in prayer position and sit quietly, focusing your gaze on the tip of the nose. Meditate or sit quietly for 3 minutes.

To End: Stand up, raise your hands above your head, and shake them. Then vigorously shake every part of your body; you may stamp your feet on the ground, kick, or dance. When this feels complete, bow gently and give thanks to the Universe.

Do this practice every day for 40 days. If you miss a day, just start over. Remember, consistency is powerful. Often, when we make changes, they are so gradual that we do not notice them. By the time we get to the endpoint, we've already forgotten how we felt at the beginning. You may wish to keep a notebook of how you feel each day so you can look back and realize the progress you've made.

Since I love quotes, I am going to close this section with one from a person who surely had every reason to have lost hope but did not. Perhaps it will give you courage, strength, and hope.

Where there's hope, there's life.
It fills us with fresh courage and makes us strong again.
— Anne Frank, *Diary of a Young Girl* —

Susan L. Atchison

Impatience

He that can have patience can have what he will.
— Benjamin Franklin —

Personal Reflections

Do you ever feel impatient? I have, many times. As a recovering "Type A" person, it's a day-to-day practice for me to be patient.

Recently, I had another opportunity to reflect on patience. I was with two friends, and we began talking about the symbolic meaning of the middle finger. Not THAT meaning—although there is a reason we use the middle finger for that. One friend said that the middle finger represents Power, which may be where the popular use of it originated. Indeed, the flasher of a middle finger likely wants to have the power to change something. The other friend said that the middle finger represents Patience. That was new to me. Putting those together, I realized that patience IS power. So, I decided to ask for Loving Insights on this.

Loving Insights

Most beautiful children, patience is the art of living in the now, the moment of time in which you take your in-breath and fill your lungs with air from the Universal Source. What is there besides this moment in time? What is there to ask for other than this? Your life will unfold in the manner in which it was planned to do, and, in this moment, you can enjoy the unfolding of it. The next moment will come in its own time, and the moment after that will follow yet you will never be anywhere except in the now. Therefore, there is no such thing as patience when you realize there is nowhere to rush off to. This is the ultimate power—that you have control of your day and your life. In your breath, give thanks for what is right now. Be here in this moment and be still in your heart. You will find that you no longer have a need to feel restless or push yourself toward some future time your busy mind had thought would fulfill you. Your fulfillment is now.

Inspired Actions: Tips and Tools for Transformation

Tips

Think about the word "impatient." It is the only word I can think of that can be transformed into its opposite so easily. Add an apostrophe and a space and "Impatient" magically becomes "I'm patient." Just by doing this, we've reclaimed our patience power.

It is good to understand that we have the power to be patient because when we are feeling impatient, we actually are giving power to people and events outside ourselves: "If only that person would hurry up!" When we focus on internal patience, we reclaim our power. Lately, I repeatedly have found myself in situations in which previously I would have been impatient, but now I find myself automatically saying to myself, "Patience is power." Somehow using those words instead of a "corrective" instruction like "I should be more patient" really works. There is a true power in it.

Tools

One of my patience personal bests is a seemingly small one. I decided that when I am driving, I will come to a FULL stop at every Stop sign. For me, that's when I completely stop the car so I feel myself move back and up in the seat a bit.

This practice has several benefits. First, not stopping fully is reinforcing the false internal belief that there is not enough time. Stopping fully affirms that I have time. (Very important for a recovering Type A person!) Second, when I fully stop and feel that slight backward and upward movement, it lifts my rib cage a bit, giving a wonderful opportunity for me to take a full, beautiful breath. Aaahh.

Find your own way to cultivate patience. It may be best to start with a simple, everyday situation as I did with the Stop signs. Imagine ahead of time how you will be patient in that situation then begin to practice it. Remember that many changes take time and lots of practice. Be patient with your patience program!

Patience is power. May you always find power in your patience.

Inspiration

Problems cannot be solved with the same mindset that created them.
— Albert Einstein —

Personal Reflections

Where does inspiration come from? Is it just random firing of our brain neurons? Or is there a bigger picture involved?

The Latin root of "inspire" is *inspirare*, which means "to breathe or blow into." In respiratory therapy, "inspiration" means the process of breathing in. In the simplest terms, it is breathing in the oxygen that feeds our brains, which then can work optimally. But is it more than that?

Loving Insights

Inspiration is the art of allowing the Light from on high to penetrate through the brain and into your heart. It is in your heart that you will find the answers; it is in your heart that you know what is true and what is right. Your brain may act as the central clearinghouse or warehouse for incoming messages, but it is the heart that knows which one to select and draw your attention.

Drop out of your everyday activities and still your mind. Your connection with All That Is cannot be clear when your mind is cluttered. If you were receiving a houseguest, you probably would clean your house or at least the areas in which your guest is going to be. You would want your home to feel clear, calm, and inviting. Likewise, you want to clean up your thoughts and smooth your neuronal chatter.

Once you have emptied your mind of unnecessary chatter, go within and state your request. What is it that you would like inspiration for? What do you wish to do with this inspiration once you receive it? Will it be for the good of humanity? It is not a bad thing for it to be good for you, too—after all, you are a part of the whole. Still, it is better if it is for the good of all. You are likely to get bigger and better ideas when you open yourself to serving others.

Now feel your heart. Become one with your heart. Does this sound strange? After all, your heart is within you, so are you not already one with it? The answer is that you are not always energetically at one with your heart. All too often your brain is going in one direction and your heart is going in another. If we had to choose, we would say to follow the direction your heart is going. Your brain can be fooled, but your heart always knows what is right.

Once you are one, envision the Light from Above coming into the top of your head. Know that it is bringing you what you wish to be inspired about. Breathe it into your heart area. Silently give thanks for all you are given. Truly, it is not you having the inspiration. It is you receiving the inspiration.

New ideas are God's way of moving humanity forward. For you to receive them is a gift from Above. Even what seems like a small idea can touch many lives.

Inspired Actions: Tips and Tools for Transformation

Tips

When I feel stuck, it helps to step away from the situation—both mentally and physically. Physical movement seems to help clear the cobwebs and allows new ideas to come in. Taking a walk is a great strategy. If you can walk in nature, so much the better.

Sometimes inspiration comes simply by the physical act of starting whatever it is that you want inspiration on. For writers, this would mean sitting down with their paper and pen or at their computer. For artists, it means picking up the paintbrush, and so forth. The simple act of starting tells the Universe to begin the flow. And so you flow!

Tools

If you need an exercise to start your flow, try writing a haiku. A haiku is a simple yet elegant poem that consists of three lines: the first line is five syllables, the second line is seven syllables, and the third line is again five syllables. Wikipedia defines it like this:

> The essence of haiku is "cutting" (*kiru*). This is often represented by the juxtaposition of two images or ideas and a *kireji* ("cutting word") between them, a kind of verbal punctuation mark that signals the moment of separation and colors the manner in which the juxtaposed elements are related.

Here are some examples:

My heart's one desire
To bring more Light to the world
Keeps me on my path

The deadline is near
I'll go take a walk outside
An idea comes

I need to decide
Which choice is right for me now
Time to meditate

What haiku might you create that illustrates your inspiration?

Join my Loving Insights Facebook group (www.facebook.com/groups/1446862912175947) and share it with me if you like.

Jealousy

Jealousy... is a mental cancer.
— B. C. Forbes —

Personal Reflections

Remember the phrase "green-eyed monster"? Jealousy is indeed a kind of a monster. Just like in the story of *Frankenstein*, once the beast is created, it is likely to turn against the one who created it—you.

Jealousy gets created when we feel inadequate compared to someone else. It's like these equations:

$$\text{I don't have X + Someone else does have X = Jealousy}$$
$$\text{I'm not Y + Someone else is Y = Jealousy}$$
$$\text{I can't do Z + Someone else can do Z = Jealousy}$$

But let's examine those equations. Who has set the standard of "adequacy"? Who has told us that we should have X, be Y, or do Z? Where did we get the message that we need those things to be happy?

Loving Insights

Most sweetest of souls, on your planet, there is an overall sense of lack and competition. This is because, going back eons, your physical selves have competed for resources. Competition means there are winners and losers. For many early cultures, being a loser meant death and not always a pleasant one. So many of you have that imprinted on your etheric field from past lives.

However, now is the time for you to clean house. Everything that was in the past can be left there. Energetically, your planet is shifting and changing, and soon you will be rising and leaving the old behind.

You can do your part in this by delving into yourself to discover whether you have any shreds of envy or jealousy hidden within. Call them out, and do not be afraid. They may look fierce or growl or even threaten to bite, but do not let this fool you. They are more afraid than you are. Put on your best coat of Light and pat them on the head. They may have been needed at one time as an indicator that you would be well advised to step it up if you wanted to make it in the world. Now that time is over. Thank them for their service and offer them a vacation because they've been on the job for a very long time! Ask them if they would like to rest and open your channel of Light to the Heaven world. Send them up to be renewed. You will feel renewed as well and lighter now that you are not carrying that burden of comparison around anymore.

Inspired Actions: Tips and Tools for Transformation

Tips

I love the Oscar Wilde quote that says, "Be yourself; everyone else is taken." It makes me laugh, but it is true. When we are feeling jealous, we are not truly being ourselves; we certainly are not honoring ourselves. Instead, we want to have, be, or do what someone else has, is, or does.

Tools

One of the most powerful mantras in the world is also one of the simplest and easiest to learn and use. Chanting "Om Mani Padme Hum" (pronounced Ohm MAH-nee PAHD-mee Hoom) is said to help transform jealousy into kindness, patience, wisdom, and compassion. A search on your favorite music source and/or YouTube will provide you with a choice of tracks to learn the pronunciation and to sing along with it. You can sing it in the car, in your home, or even silently while at work or out and about.

To really dedicate yourself to rooting out jealousy, buy yourself a "mala" (a special necklace made with 108 beads). You use the beads to count repetitions of whatever mantra you are doing—in this case, the Om Mani Padme Hum. Using the beads gives you a tactile sense (you touch one bead for each repetition then move to the next one) and allows you to focus on the intention and energy of the mantra rather than the counting of them. Repeat the mantra 108 times each day for at least 40 days. If you skip a day before you reach 40 consecutive days, start over.

Given that jealousy is so old, as the Loving Insights wisdom has told us, it is possible that it might take a while to root out. If you discover you have a jealous feeling, don't berate yourself for it. (As if that would help!)

Instead, feed your brain with positive affirmations about yourself:

> I am me.
> I am the only me there is.
> I am safe to be me.
> I love being me!
> Being me keeps getting better and better.
> I am excited about me.
> I love me… I love me… I love me.

Joy

*We are shaped by our thoughts; we become what we think.
When the mind is pure, joy follows like a shadow that never leaves.*
— Buddha —

Personal Reflections

Joy is the ultimate goal, isn't it? Or is it? Living in joy certainly sounds desirable and wonderful. Yet some people say that it is not possible to live in joy and that we should live in contentment or happiness instead. What do you think? Is the feeling of joy like a drug—leaving us wanting and chasing more? Or is it our natural state?

Reflect on the times in your life when you have felt joy. As I look back over my life, there were a few times when I felt joy or a kind of super-contentment. Two of those times were so simple—each happened while I was walking through a neighborhood observing nature. In one, I walked under a very large maple tree as a strong breeze launched a cloud of V-shaped silvery seed pods, which cascaded down in a shimmery shower of twirling delights all around me. The other time, I was walking by an empty, overgrown lot. It was dusk on a foggy day, and the lot was filled with fireflies winking on and off in the mist. Both times, as I was immersed in such beauty, I felt as if life could be complete right then and that would be fine. For me, this felt more like joy than human activities did because graduating, getting a job, getting married, and so on, all seem to have so many other emotions, expectations, and attachments with them. In those two nature experiences, I was just right there, in the moment, feeling the absolute beauty and joy of life.

Loving Insights

Joy is your birthright and natural home; however, it is not the joy you feel when you achieve a goal in life. Rather, it is the sweet, soft joy of being alive, of knowing that you are one part of the whole, of looking around the great web of life and seeing all the beautiful connections in every direction, of knowing that the unfathomable love of your Creator is available to you at any moment.

Joy is found in helping, serving, and sharing the gifts of Light with others. Joy is within you, not without you. All the outer aspects you have thought would bring you joy can change. The house, car, marriage, children, health… these all are markers or signposts in life; they are not the reasons for life.

Be present in this moment—this very moment. Feel your breath coming in and out. Notice the sweet, soft smile at the edges of your mouth. Feel the air on your skin. Imagine that you can feel the blood flowing through your veins and arteries and your stomach digesting food for you. You have an entire factory going on inside you at all times—you are the CEO of the most amazing enterprise ever created!

Feel the beginnings of joy as if it is a clear, small flame just beginning to grow. Appreciation is the oxygen that feeds this flame. Find appreciation in every aspect of your life. Appreciate the Sun, the wind, the Moon, the clouds, the sky, the Earth. Look around you and find your joy. It is there all along.

Inspired Actions: Tips and Tools for Transformation

Tips

When you water and care for your plants, they grow. When you feed and nurture your children, they grow. Whatever we pay attention to grows. So, let's pay attention to the joy that is present in our lives.

That may mean that we need to look for it. I start each day by going out on my kitchen deck to pray, chant, and offer food to the birds and animals. There is great joy for me in seeing the chickadees, blue jays, cardinals, juncos, chipmunks, and squirrels gather to enjoy their seeds. If I did not do this, these birds and critters would still be in the neighborhood, but they would not have gathered at my deck. Thus, by my giving, I am calling in joy.

Where might there be joy in your life that you can call in?

Tools

What if you can find joy in your everyday life? Go outside—is it cloudy? What joy can you find in that? Is it sunny? Does that make you feel joy? How about snow or rain?

We can use many of the same tools we use for gratitude to bring our attention to the joy in life:

- Joy Jar—Get a large jar. Each day, write down on a slip of paper something in which you found joy. Put the paper in the jar. You can review these periodically.
- Joy Journal—Write about your journey to joy, including all the moments in which you discovered joy.
- Joyful Pause—Set your phone alarm. When it goes off, pause to find a moment of joy.

Where your attention goes, your energy and emotions tend to follow. Be the CEO, the leader of your own ship. Set a course for Destination Joy.

Judgment

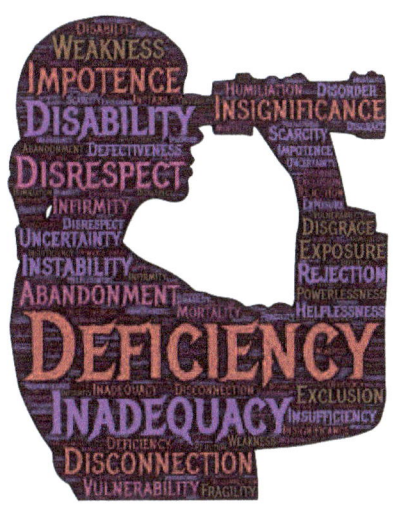 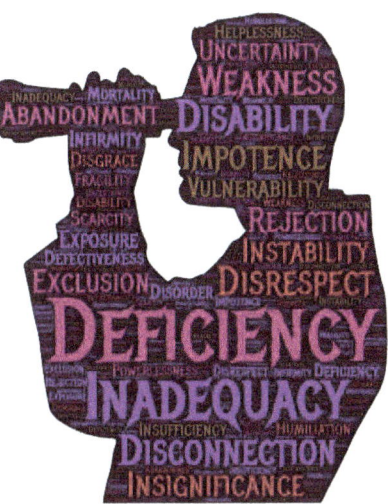

*As I get older, the more I stay focused on
the acceptance of myself and others and
choose compassion over judgment and curiosity over fear.*
— Tracee Ellis Ross —

Personal Reflections

Judging is really labeling. Labels can be useful. Without them, how would we know which can of soup to reach for? Labels serve as a kind of shorthand way to categorize things or people.

In the therapy world, we understand that a diagnosis, such as "depression, moderate, recurrent" means that the person is experiencing a fairly standard set of symptoms. This allows us to focus on a short list, which saves time and can help us be effective.

However, the very use of a label also can exclude the whole multidimensional person. This is one of the reasons I have chosen not to be affiliated with any insurance companies. It frees me to skip the check-box diagnosis and devote myself to the whole person.

In the generation and family in which I grew up, labeling and categorizing was common. We lived with my grandmother while I was a child, so I got to know her pretty well. Grandma had many wonderful qualities. She was a hard worker (as a teacher in a one-room schoolhouse to which she would need to go early to start the fire in the potbelly stove so they would have heat), a pretty good cook (we still love her spaghetti casserole recipe), and smart enough to be a good bridge player and stay well informed by reading two newspapers every day. I can only hope I have inherited some of her wonderful qualities.

Like many people in her generation, Grandma's first response when she saw or heard about someone was to ask a labeling or categorizing question like, "What nationality is he?" or "How old is she?" But, also like many people in her generation—and sadly in ours, too—her brain had been trained to take the next step after labeling and categorizing to judging.

When does labeling and categorizing become judging? I believe it is when there is a "good" and/or "bad" attached to the label. Grandma would follow up the "category" questions with comments on the person's appearance or what she perceived their personal characteristics might be. (When she got older and deafer, she would do this loudly in public, which could be somewhat embarrassing for those with her.)

It's not something that's easy to admit, but I sometimes found myself thinking along Grandma's lines. As a young adult, it worried me that the way she had been taught to judge was passed onto me. So, in my early 20s, I made a conscious decision to focus on what is good and admirable about each person I met. While this was a challenge at first, I persevered, and it became a natural way of being (or thinking). It sure feels better than the old way!

Loving Insights

Recently, I was channeling the Loving Insights voice to provide guidance for someone, and that voice asked the question, "Why is she judging herself?" Inspired by the question posed to this person, I decided to ask, "Please teach me about judgment." We had a short dialogue:

> **Loving Insights:** Most precious and holy child, I am with you always. Beloved, your world has divided itself into categories and subcategories, on and on until the smallest parameter is reached. In these, you place yourself as if in a restraining cubicle. As you look around, you see neither sideways nor backward, only in front of you. How you have misused your ability to connect with those around you. Beloved, when you place someone in a cubbyhole, you no longer have connection with them. As each person is a part of Me, you then lose connection with All That Is. The sweetness of life is drained away. When you observe a person, a situation, or an event, my precious children, I ask you to see through the eyes of the beloved.
>
> **Me:** So, if people are in cubbyholes, then some are above and some are below; some are far away and some are closer.
>
> **LI:** Thus, you are deceiving yourself, for truly all souls are equal in the eyes of the Lord. You see a fraction of a moment of a soul's life. How can you judge on this? It is as if you were looking through a pinhole in a window. A covering is over your own eyes. As you purify yourself, you slowly remove that dark covering, and behold, the true picture begins to emerge.
>
> **Me:** It feels better to me when, as I look at or think about someone, I focus on all the qualities that I like about them.
>
> **LI:** As you do this, you will widen the lens through which you are looking. For truly, all are loved.

Susan L. Atchison

Inspired Actions: Tips and Tools for Transformation

Tips

Judgment can be insidious. Despite my best efforts, I still find it creeping into my thinking. Usually, it is related to something that I feel inadequate or insecure about in myself. For a while, I was sensitive about the size of my nose, which I judged as "too big," and my chin, which I judged as "too small." During that time, I noticed every other woman's nose and chin. It's as if that judging thought sprang into my mind without my permission! Then I needed to work to evict it. This was a real battle for me.

However, this battle to control our minds is nothing new in the world, and I can take wisdom from the Native American culture, as in this beautiful traditional story:

> An old Cherokee told his grandchild, "Child, there is a battle between two wolves inside us all. One is Evil. It is anger, envy, jealousy, sorrow, regret, greed, arrogance, self-pity, guilt, resentment, inferiority, lies, false pride, superiority, and ego. The other is Good. It is joy, peace, love, hope, serenity, humility, kindness, benevolence, empathy, generosity, truth, compassion, and faith."
>
> The grandchild thought about it and asked, "Grandfather, which wolf wins?"
>
> The old man quietly replied, "The one you feed."

Tools

Imagine that you have a pen in your hand. You can use that pen to write an inspirational story, a beautiful poem, a mystery, a recipe, a laundry list, a critical letter, an inflammatory article, or a kidnapping note. Your mind is like that pen—you have complete choice about how to think about someone or something and what you will create with those thoughts.

If your mind has been in the habit of judging others, gradually introduce it to another way of being. When you see someone whom your mind would judge, instead find at least one thing about that person that you can appreciate, honor, or commend. It doesn't even have to be something you like.

For instance, let's say someone is wearing clothing that you think is ridiculous, too baggy, too tight, or too skimpy. Just try this on instead. Admire that person's creativity, willingness to go outside the norm to express themselves, or their sense of fun in life. If you need to, you can even imagine you are erasing the old judgmental statement and writing over it with the new thought.

Another way to redirect judgmental thoughts is to play the "What If" game. For instance, if you are at a stoplight and the person behind you is honking their horn before you've even had a chance to move your foot from the brake to the gas, you could judge them as impatient, self-centered, or something worse. Or you could say, "What if… he has sick kids in the car? What if… her mother just died? What if… this driver just got a phone call saying their teenager has been picked up by the cops?"

As you continue to do this, you are training your brain to change the immediate thoughts it holds. After a while, the new way will become second nature to you, and you will feel better. Your better-feeling state will radiate out to those around you, and you will find yourself having a happier life.

Susan L. Atchison

Laziness

There is a great volcano sleeping in every laziness!
— Mehmet Murat Ildan —

Personal Reflections

It seems that these days "laziness" is used as a kind of a put-down for people or even entire cultures. It's just another way of dividing ourselves, saying that we are "better" than those other people. This one is based on an outlook that work and achievement are the most important things in life, or at least keeping busy is.

I know that sometimes I have felt lazy and did not want to keep on keeping busy—or was it that I needed some downtime, or maybe that whatever I was "supposed" to be doing wasn't ready to "be done"? How do you tell the difference?

Loving Insights

Sweetest of souls, we have come to the topic of laziness, which your people apply to others more than to themselves and do so in an effort to put the others down while congratulating themselves inordinately for their own efforts.

Laziness is fear, and fear is pervasive throughout your world. Laziness is the unwillingness to face what might be if effort were put forth. This can solidify into a habitual pattern just as when sludge gets created and becomes difficult to move through. Another metaphor you might like is that of quicksand. At first, you are only in it up to your ankles, but if you don't extricate yourself from it, it gradually will suck you down until you are completely immobilized.

The antidote for laziness is not more effort but more confidence. We can help each other have more confidence by finding something we like about the other and offering supportive words about that. Those words land like soft butterflies on an individual. Gradually over time, those butterflies will have the strength to help that individual up and out of the sludge in which they were lost.

We all should do this routinely because who among you does not need some validation or positive feedback? Humans are wired to be social animals, and together you are stronger than you are alone.

So, when you see someone who you might think of as lazy, challenge your own mind to find a positive aspect about them. Even if you are reading about this person or seeing them in a news report, send positive, loving, and uplifting energies to them. Your efforts will not go to waste because all positive blessings lift the energies of the entire world.

Inspired Actions: Tips and Tools for Transformation

Tips

Every day, search your mind to see if there is someone, or some group of people, that you are labeling or condemning as "lazy." Now imagine being in their shoes, with only the resources they have—not your resources (physical, mental, emotional, financial, educational, communal), but theirs. I love the Loving Insights idea of blessings and uplifting thoughts being sent out as butterflies. Send butterflies of blessings to them to uplift them and bring them new resources that will give them exactly what they need. Notice how this makes you feel. Is it a different feeling than when you just condemned them as lazy?

Some of you may be familiar with Maslow's Hierarchy of Needs. This is a pyramid that demonstrates how people tend to move upward from their basic needs, such as food and shelter, to more self-actualizing needs, such as creative pursuits. The pyramid is wider at the bottom because the basic needs are many and varied and narrower at the top because the needs become more refined. Some might say that the pyramid also is wider at the bottom because more people are in those stages of development.

As I was thinking about this one day, it occurred to me that this Hierarchy of Needs does not exist in a vacuum. Systems theory tells us that we need to account for all the factors around the situation. An image popped into my head that we should surround the pyramid with a "container" of potential energy and resources available at each stage. It seems logical that when a person's attention is consumed by just being able to obtain their basic needs, there is not much left for self-development. So, I created the following model to depict this. It may help us understand and be compassionate to those who are struggling on the "lower" levels.

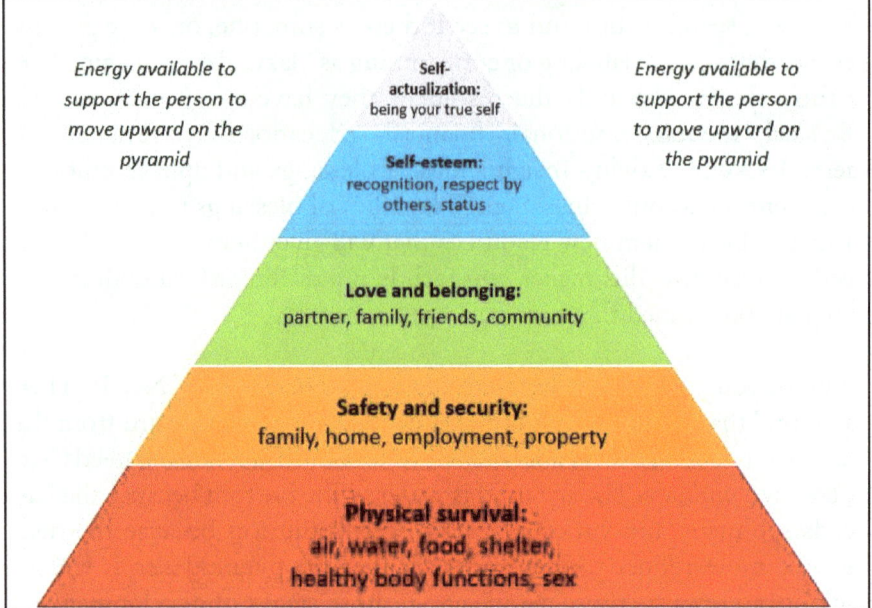

Tools

If you have been labeling yourself—or someone else—as lazy, try this instead. Ask yourself to T.H.I.N.K. first. That is, ask if this thought or statement is True, Helpful, Inspiring, Necessary, and Kind.

To help you assess whether your thought or statement is true, you can apply Byron Katie's formula (from http://thework.com/en/do-work):

1. Is it true? (Yes or no. If no, move to Question 3.)
2. Can you absolutely know it's true? (Yes or no.)
3. How do you react, and what happens, when you believe that thought?
4. Who would you be without the thought?

Be absolutely honest with yourself while working through these questions.

In the section on Anxiety, we discuss the classic yogic pranayama (breathing) exercise of "Left Nostril Breathing" for soothing yourself. Now you can utilize "Right Nostril Breathing" to invigorate yourself. Just close off your left nostril with your thumb and inhale through the right nostril. Then, still with the left nostril closed, exhale only through the right nostril. Repeat this about 10 times. Right Nostril Breathing energizes you.

Once you have reinvigorated yourself, take one small action. Fear left on its own tends to feed on itself and grow, but actions have a way of breaking you out of that cycle. Action dispels fear. Try it now.

Susan L. Atchison

Loneliness

When we are most alone is when we embrace another's loneliness.
— Mitch Albom —

Personal Reflections

Few experiences seem more difficult for my clients than loneliness. We are wired for connection. As babies, connection is survival. As adults, connection is support; it allows us to both give and receive.

Sometimes people feel lonely because those around them don't seem to understand them. This often seems to happen when you are starting on a path of spiritual awakening. Your family and friends no longer have as many similarities with you as before. They are unable to understand, and may not even be interested in, your new focus. So, just at the time you'd like to share and talk about your exciting new awareness, it often seems like there is no one there for you.

As we go through life, we find ourselves around people who resonate with us at the time. But life is growth, and people will grow in different directions. Each of us is like a plant, growing toward its own sunlight. It is natural that, as you lean toward your source of Light, you may be leaning in a different direction than even the plants closest to you.

Loving Insights

Most beautiful ones, loneliness is the cruelest cut of all because all your other maladies—jealousy, depression, hurt, and fear—can be remedied by being with others who understand. But when you feel you have no one who understands, you are left with all those burdens AND with loneliness. It is a double whammy.

Yet loneliness has been given as a gift to humanity to help you understand what is important and in which direction to move. If you are lonely when you're with others, this is your sign that it is time for you to put out the call for the Universe to bring you in connection with those who are more "on your wavelength."

If you are lonely because you are truly alone, you can use this time to delve more deeply into your own self. Sit with yourself until you are comfortable with yourself and you are not so much needing someone to fill you as you are wanting to share with others. Others can feel the difference between a person who wants something from them and a person who is sharing with them.

Know, too, that life tends to run in cycles. When you view your loneliness as a part of the cycle, it may be less upsetting to you. Decide what it is you want instead of this feeling of loneliness and ask for help in moving toward that destination. Then be open to how the Universe responds. It may not be in the way you had imagined at all, but it will be in the way that is just right for you.

Inspired Actions: Tips and Tools for Transformation

Tips

First, figure out what or whom it is you are lonely for. You might be lonely for a specific person; for likeminded people who accept, support, and guide you on your journey; for companionship in general; for the existence of meaning in your life, or for a more felt sense of connection with your Creator. Usually, connection is the key. Where in your life are you wanting to connect or reconnect?

Next, decide what one small step you can take to bring that into your life. Are you looking for a person with whom to have a romantic relationship? A spiritual community? Or maybe just some friends? Share your interests with those around you; you never know what this might open up.

Tools

Be sure to get enough sleep. Research has shown a correlation between the lack of adequate sleep and feelings of loneliness. (A link to this research is in the Resources section.)

Take the action of trying something new. Go to a new place or be with new people. True, this will not always work out, but when you do this, you are gaining experience and having an opportunity to have some fun. To alleviate concerns about this new experience working out, try thinking of it as an experiment. You are simply experimenting being in this place, in this situation, or with these people. Plus, it sets your intention and the energy in motion. Each time you take a step, it reinforces your intentions and energy and "instructs" the Universe to bring more to you.

Every morning, ask the Universe to help you on this journey, and hold to your vision of yourself feeling happy and connected with the perfect right people.

Susan L. Atchison

Love

Your task is not to seek for love but merely to seek and find all the barriers within yourself that you have built against it.
— Rumi —

Personal Reflections

Love! The epitome of all topics. Surely there has been more than enough written about love to last lifetimes. But when I asked people what topics they would like included in this book, "Love" was the #1 response. We need love, we want love, we, well, love love.

So, what do we need to know about love?

Loving Insights

Your true nature is to live in love, to express love, to feel love, to be loved. Your body emits love as it does light—in truth they are one and the same. There can be no darkness where there is light, and there can be no pain, fear, or death where there is love. Love transcends all else. Your Creator made you in love and maintains you in love.

For many thousands of years, humanity has lost its way and turned its back on love. Even love of family is limited love. It is but a taste of the true love for all that your Creator endowed in you and that which you are indeed capable of resurrecting. Do you love everyone around you? You do not need to wish to bring them home for lunch to feel great love for them because love accepts a person just as they are. Love understands. Love forgives. Love allows. What a great gift this is, to allow each person to be just who they are at that moment. In the next moment, both you and this other person will be changed.

How can you begin to blow on the ember of love embedded in your heart? First, bring the love of your Creator to the forefront. Each and every day, take a few moments to dedicate yourself to living, as best as you can, for your Creator's honor. Next, send loving thoughts to all around you. This is easy to do but also easy to forget.

What actions can you take that will demonstrate love to those around you? Sharing, giving, helping… all these are outward manifestations of your internal love. Feel the love. Give the love. Be the love.

Inspired Actions: Tips and Tools for Transformation

Tips

How often can we bring our minds back to thinking loving thoughts about people? For me, this is like a living meditation. Those people in front of me in line taking a REALLY long time to transact their business? Well, that could be—and sometimes is—me. So, I can send loving thoughts to them and to myself. Plus, I remind myself that this business would not be here for me, nor would the roads to get here, without all the other customers who come here. So, then I can bless them for making my life so much easier.

Tools

So often we are advised that we need to love ourselves in order to love others. Sometimes it seems as though it is easier to love others. Following is an exercise I recommend to my clients to help open them to loving themselves.

Stand in front of the mirror. Look yourself in the eyes. Now say "I love you" nine times. You don't need to believe it yet—just say it to observe and experience how you feel with each repetition. I could tell you how it feels for me as I go through the nine repetitions, but I'd rather you experience it for yourself. Go do it now.

- What was that like for you? Can you do this every day, at least once?
- Now, can you also mentally say "I love you" to the people around you?
- Next, extend that love to people with whom you have difficulty.

Finally, send your love out to the whole world. Here's a lovely way to do this:

Hold your hands out together in front of you, palms up.

Imagine a small flame in the center of your palms.

Breathe gently on it as you would to help an ember glow,
infusing the flame with whatever blessing(s) you wish for our world,
such as peace, love, joy, prosperity, compassion, freedom, and so on.

Breathe on the flame again to help it glow bigger and brighter.

Now bring your palms up by your lips.

Take a big inhale and then, as you exhale,
blow that flame with its blessings out to the world.

Numbness

Numb the dark and you numb the light.
— Brené Brown —

Personal Reflections

Have you ever been so stressed that you just became numb? Like you don't feel anything anymore? Some emotions, such as anxiety and depression, can feel so difficult that being numb might sometimes feel like a better choice. But it's not really a conscious choice—it's our nervous system shutting down to protect us. It's similar to when an animal in the wild is wounded and goes into a secluded place to basically shut down until its body can recuperate.

As protective as it might be, when we're numb, not only are we not feeling hurt and pain, but we're also not feeling happiness or love. Like the leaf in the photo, we are disconnected, cold, and alone and can even feel lifeless. Sometimes this seems like a decent tradeoff. I've had clients who are recovering from trauma-induced numbness get mad at me because the therapy they are doing is giving them what they asked for, which is a fuller life. But that fuller life, at least at first, includes hurt and pain as well as happiness and love. Often the hurt and pain surface first, so it's understandable that this doesn't feel good. But as these emotions are cleared, it opens the space for love, happiness, and even joy.

Loving Insights

Beloveds, your physical system is not a lightbulb that turns on and off; rather it is a riverbed that holds more or less water. The river and its surroundings will operate at an optimal level when the water flowing through it is good, clean, and at the right volume. If there is too little water, it will not flow easily enough to carry away debris and you will likely notice that not only is it not nourishing the land around it, but it is perhaps becoming slimy and overgrown. On the other hand, a riverbed that has too much water flowing through it will take down what is growing around it. Nothing will get nourished then either because the water will be too strong to gently pause so plants and animals can have a drink. Likewise, you have an optimal level at which your systems will operate. Too little, and you will become stagnant and unnourished. Too much, and you will be overwhelmed and also unnourished.

Therefore, be mindful of the energy you are funneling into your system. Be sure you have an adequate, clean channel for it to run through as well as a proper place for it to empty. Do your meditations and prayers, not just to obtain something new for yourself but also to regularly maintain that clean flow through you. In this way, you will be nourished, and your energy will be able to expand and contract a bit—as healthy organisms do—without impediment.

Inspired Actions: Tips and Tools for Transformation

Tips

When you are feeling numb, often almost any suggestion to help move you to a better place can feel overwhelming. So, it may be best to start with something small or easy—baby steps, as they say.

Often holding something warm can feel nurturing when you are feeling numb. There are teddy bears into which you can put heat packs. Even taking socks or a sweater from the dryer feels good. Holding a cup of coffee or tea can begin to restore you to life.

Tools

Essential oils, with their exceptionally small molecules, have a remarkable ability to dispel numbness. After being inhaled, the molecules go directly to the amygdala, a cluster of neurons that manages emotions, such as anxiety. Once there, the molecules of essential oils begin to unwind the fear response throughout your nervous system, thus dispersing the numbness and restoring a fuller sense of being.

Essential oils especially supportive in this regard include black pepper, cistus, frankincense, and ginger (notice that these tend to be "warm" oils). Just put a drop in your hands, rub your palms together, hold your palms up to your nose, and inhale deeply. You might want to rub a drop on the back of your neck and onto your occiput, which is the curve at the base of your skull. Remember that every nerve in your body runs through your neck, so applying oils to the spine at your neck can positively affect your entire body.

"Grounding" (which is also known as "earthing") is an easy way to come out of numbness. Grounding is when you align with the Earth's electrons. You know how you can feel better while on the sand or in ocean water? Both sand and salt water are wonderful conductors of Earth energy. Other ways to ground include walking barefoot, or in shoes with natural leather soles, on dirt, grass, or concrete. You also could purchase a grounding mat or sheet for your bed. A more budget-friendly solution could be getting a pan big enough for your feet and filling it with sand. Sit each day with your feet in the sand.

I ground myself each morning by walking out on our wooden deck to feed the birds, chant, and pray. If it is cold, I wear shoes with leather soles because that conducts the Earth's energies. Just those few moments of standing outside, offering sustenance to the wildlife and my prayers for the world while taking in the beauty of the trees and the Sun coming up, fuels me for the day.

What simple step can you take?

Oneness

*The essence of spirituality is to be constantly aware
of the oneness of all;
at the same time to celebrate the uniqueness of the individual.*
— Jaggi Vasudev —

Personal Reflections

Oneness—it's the big spiritual topic of the day. It's said to be both our source and our goal. We are one with everything and everyone in the Universe.

This sounds really spiritual, doesn't it? But what does it really mean in a practical, everyday sort of way? I mean, I don't know about you, but there certainly are some things—and some people—that I am quite sure I do not wish to be "one" with! And I believe that I have invested quite a bit of energy through the years toward staying separate from others—sometimes even those close to me.

Oneness can be scary. For some people—especially those who were hurt by the ones they loved and depended on—the thing that they want and need most (emotional intimacy) is also the very thing of which they are the most frightened. And aren't some of us also like that with spiritual Oneness?

Loving Insights

Radiant ones, there really is no other topic than oneness. Once you have oneness "down," you've got all the rest of it covered, for you are one with All That Is. There is nothing in the Universe of which you are not a part and which is not a part of you. You are made from the same molecules that have been or will be in the far-off stars. You are one with Me and one with each other.

It is a human condition to attempt to separate yourselves from Me, from the Earth, from the flora and fauna, and from each other. But it is just a trick—nothing more than that—for in truth there is no separation. I give you the Earth, the stars, the Sun, the Moon, and the air that you breathe. You are not separate from any of it. Nor are you separate from each other. You all have the same emotions—you feel anger, fear, hurt, pain, disappointment, excitement, and joy. You just think you feel them about different things. But at the heart of it, it is the same for each of you.

What would it be like for you to truly understand that you are one with Me and one with All That Is? How would you live your life differently if you knew that you were born from Me and will return to Me? You are vibrating particles of energy—as is everything else that you see, hear, or feel in your world. There are no barriers in energy; energy passes through walls, through the forest, through the air, through the world. Your energy is My energy.

Sit now and allow yourself to become one with all that is. Feel the vibrations of the energy that flows from Me, through everything else in your world and beyond, and into you then back in an endless loop. You are One.

Inspired Actions: Tips and Tools for Transformation

Tips

The word *bindu* means "point." It also can be thought of as a seed. A seed is a single, often very small (think of the mustard seed in the Bible) point from which much can arise. As Ralph Waldo Emerson said, "The creation of a thousand forests is in one acorn."

Metaphysically, bindu is held to be the point at which begins creation—from which all experiences arise—and the point at which the many come together again into unity.

In the classic yin-yang symbol, you will see that there are two separate parts. Yet each part has a bindu of the other within it.

Tools

Sit quietly in a meditative spot. You may wish to have a journal or art materials nearby.

Think of something you have considered as being separate from you. It may be best to start with something small. For this introduction, we will use a blade of grass as an example. Allow yourself to be the gold portion of the yin-yang symbol and this blade of grass to be the white portion. Now reflect on the bindu (the white dot inside the gold) of the grass within you. What aspect or qualities of the blade of grass do you also have?

Do you require nourishment from the Earth? From the Sun? Do you take in the oxygen it provides and use it for life? Do you bounce back after being walked on? Do you give beauty and a comforting place for those around you? Then think of what the bindu of you (the gold dot within the white) in the blade of grass represents. Does it take in the carbon dioxide that you exhale and use it as nourishment?

Go further. Think of someone or something you have considered to be separate from you. It may be a difficult person, an organization that holds opposite views, or perhaps even an entire culture that has mystified or even repelled you. Again, allow yourself to be the gold portion, and this "other" to be the white portion, and meditate on the bindu in each. Do you care for your family? Do they care for their families? Do you breathe the same air—even if it travels a long way? Do you have similar fears? Keep reflecting on this until you have discovered at least three points of similarity.

You can train your mind to use this process to remind yourself again and again of how you are, indeed, one with all there is. Our egos like to pretend we are separate. The Divine Mind knows we are One.

Rage

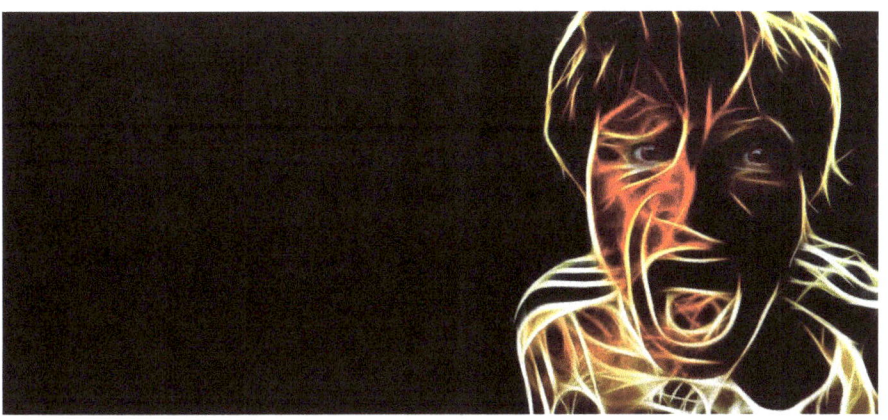

Rage is the truest path to chaos.
— Kevin J Kessler —

Personal Reflections

Whenever a writer is unsure about how to begin something, using the dictionary to define the topic is a good start. It's like taking a deep breath before answering a question; it buys you some time to think. Have you guessed that I didn't know where to start with the topic of Rage? So, here we go. Here's the dictionary definition:

> Merriam Webster (www.merriam-webster.com) defines "rage" as:
> 1. violent and uncontrolled anger
> 2. a fit of violent wrath
> 3. violent action (as of wind or sea)
> 4. an intense feeling: passion
> 5. a fad pursued with intense enthusiasm

The common denominator among these definitions seems to be the level of intensity inherent in rage. Rage is anger on steroids. Anger can be a useful emotion to get us moving, particularly in threatening situations. So, rage would be what's needed when plain ol' vanilla anger won't do the trick. Rage is like the energy a mother uses to lift a car off her child. Rage was designed to move mountains—or perhaps more specifically to power a person facing seemingly insurmountable odds, like fighting off an invader. So maybe rage had, or still has, a useful purpose? Think about soldiers going into war, particularly in the days of hand-to-hand combat. Rage could be a helpful—and even necessary—emotion then.

Loving Insights

Divine children, when a fire has been smoldering for a long time, it may suddenly leap up into a powerful blast, given the right circumstances and combination of fuels. A sudden influx of oxygen, access to a flammable material—and pow! The smoldering fire becomes a raging inferno. Similarly, rage often does not come out of nowhere; rather it has been smoldering at a low level for some time, waiting for the very thing that will set it off. This is the reason you are encouraged to continually do meditation, cleanse your chakras, chant, and pray. You are decreasing the fuel for explosions as well as making yourselves happier and calmer in the process.

An individual who is prone to rage must examine the underlying aspects. Is their nutrition off? Have their traumas been explored and acknowledged and has healing work begun? Is their brain or nervous system on overload? Do they have support of family, friends, a social circle, a spiritual group? Rage is a last resort for many people when they are feeling threatened and alone.

Rage is not to be trifled with; a person in the middle of rage cannot think and cannot be reasoned with. If you are with someone who is raging, create safety for yourself first and later ask if there is a way to help the rager feel safer. But that person must do their own work, too. Do not try to rescue a rager—that will lead only to disappointment and hurt for you as well as add more fuel to their fire. Instead, find your own safe place then you can direct them to places more equipped to handle explosives.

Inspired Actions: Tips and Tools for Transformation

Tips

If you have a rager in your life, your first responsibility is to create safety for yourself, as the Loving Insights suggest. Once you are in a safe place, you can direct your prayers and meditations to help lift the burden from this individual. You also can, when you go to bed and just before you go to sleep, ask that the person be taken during their sleep time to "Wisdom School" (a place on another level of consciousness or energy) to learn healthy new ways to manage their fear and anger. You also can envision any unhealthy cords or ties connecting you to this person. See an angel coming down to dissolve that energetic connection. Ask for healing to be given for the highest good of all.

Tools

If you are the person suffering with rage, you must begin to meditate—every day, even if for only a few minutes. When you meditate, try to envision the fire that has been burning or smoldering in you. Acknowledge it. Ask what lesson it has been trying to teach you. Let anything come into your mind. You may do this many times and get many different answers; over time, you will come to learn and understand which ones are the most meaningful for you. Again, acknowledge that lesson. Ask how you can manage this aspect of your life in a more productive manner. Ask to be guided and assisted in this. You may be guided to books, podcasts, webinars, seminars, or professionals to help you relieve yourself of the burden of rage. Know that you can do it, and that, when you emerge from the fire, you will be stronger and will have given much to the healing of the world as well.

A more physically active tool is to trance dance. This is when you create a safe space—about a 3- by 5-foot spot—in which you can dance with your eyes closed. A yoga mat or area rug is about the right size. To trance dance, find some powerful drumming music. (The Professor Trance and the Energisers collection, Shaman's Breath, is ideal for this.) Take your shoes off so you can feel the edges of your yoga mat or area rug; this will keep you in your safe zone. Put on the music, close your eyes, and let your body move to the beat. Set your intention beforehand that you will be freeing rage from your body in a healthy, positive way. Then let your body shake off that rage energy.

Afterward, you may wish to take a bath with sea salt to complete the cleansing of your energy field. Then bring some positive energy in by massaging your body with lavender and/or frankincense oil in an organic vegetable oil base, drinking lemon water, or going for a walk in nature.

Rebelliousness

*Only true rebelliousness can change the world for the better.
Be rebellious.*
— Debasish Mridha —

Personal Reflections

Were you ever rebellious? Maybe as a teen? I know I was! Ducking out of school (even finding ways to get out of and then back into a "closed" campus), going places I shouldn't have been, experimenting with drugs, lying to my parents, dropping out of college to live with my boyfriend in the basement of an old house—yep, just about the whole nine yards.

Even as an adult, I've been rebellious in various ways. I couldn't just study the typical talk therapy—I had to learn hypnotherapy, past-life therapy, and even how to do depossessions (not as hard as you might think). Because life has a beautiful way of bringing us into balance, I now find that the typical therapy practice of simply sitting and listening to people is one of my favorite ways to work. And it is much needed—there is a desperate thirst in people to have someone truly and deeply listen to and understand them.

I also was one of the first to leave my long-time spiritual "Mystery" school. Interestingly, on the first day of that school, as the teacher talked about how some of us ultimately would leave the group and that a few of those who left would leave in anger, I had a sinking feeling inside that this was likely to be me. Sometimes I would strike out on a new path, but sometimes I would just strike out against someone or something.

Where did this rebelliousness come from? On a psychological level, it's probably pretty easy to trace back. My grandmother, with whom we lived, needed to be super controlling of everything (see the section on Judgment). My dad had undiagnosed depression and sometimes took it out in anger at me and my sister (see the section on Anger). My mother was often sort of a non-presence—there in body but not really in other ways. I often felt as though my role was to make everything okay for everybody. Not only is this not possible, but it ignored my own needs. Not surprisingly, I was frustrated, angry, and resentful, so I rebelled. But too often, the rebellion was really manifested anger at people or rules that, consciously or subconsciously, reminded me of the authorities in my family.

On another level, it couldn't have been just my family dynamics. My older sister grew up in the very same family yet she never rebelled a day in her life (that I know of). She always has been unfailingly practical, sweet, and kind. Maybe I can (or should) lay it at the feet of being a Scorpio—feeling things intensely?

Loving Insights

Child of mine, there is a time and a place for rebelliousness. Without rebelliousness, civilization would not have moved forward. Someone has to be the first to step out of the established paradigm and into new territory whether that territory is physical, mental, or spiritual. This is called proactive rebellion.

Consider the many revered stories about people, such as Martin Luther and Malala Yousafzai, who have done this. Others acted in a rebellious way and, although ultimately celebrated, they were not initially well received, such as Nelson Mandela, Martin Luther King, Jr., and Susan B. Anthony. Add to that whistleblowers and those who report abuse of any kind—very often their rebellion is discounted, dismissed, or even defamed.

Then there is rebellion born in the psyche rather than the soul. This is human rebellion. Often, this is a reaction to a perceived lack of control or anger at a person or institution seen as being in control when they should not be. Rather than a person having a desire to bring out truth, or to move in the direction of truth, they are rejecting and moving away from someone or something primarily for the reason of "showing them up."

You can tell the difference by the anger underneath. A person being called by their soul to create something new initially might have anger about the inequality of an existing paradigm, but this anger dissipates and is replaced by the desire to birth a new way of being. The focus is on the future, on an envisioned goal that is good for all.

The person who is rebellious for the sake of being rebellious does not have that dream or vision in their heart. Rather, this person is focused on the perceived unfairness or inequality of the existing situation and the people or institutions in charge. Their focus is on the rebellion itself. Do you see the difference? This kind of rebellion likely will lead nowhere because it is facing the past rather than the future. The most it will do is go in a circle.

True rebellion is known in the heart and soul. It is an action that the person knows she or he needs to take, regardless of the possible consequences.

Inspired Actions: Tips and Tools for Transformation

Tips

How do we know when we are being rebellious in a reactive way and when we are being rebellious in a proactive way? I think the Loving Insights message got it just right. Healthy rebellion is forward looking—again, that's proactive—and has a vision of a worthy goal while unhealthy rebellion is reactive—targeted at those who you think did you wrong.

Tools

When you are feeling rebellious, sit quietly (or as quietly as might be possible under your circumstances) and notice which way your rebelliousness is facing.

If you notice that your rebelliousness is facing backward, or toward a person or an institution, follow that thread in as much of a nonjudgmental way (including judgment of yourself) as you can. Ask to be shown, or to understand, the source of this reactive rebellion. Let yourself feel the emotions that may come up while you have thoughts or memories of situations that may have contributed toward this rebellion.

Then find your own way to dissipate these emotions. You might write them down then tear up or burn the papers. You might imagine yourself with a draft of an old screenplay with that scene on it then simply going to the computer and deleting it and writing a new, more satisfying scene. You might infuse the new scene with Light. You can even go and talk it over with a trusted friend, spiritual advisor, or counselor. Whatever way you decide will be the perfect right one for you.

Now replace it with proactive rebellion. Was there some hurt or unfairness in whatever generated your reactive rebellion with which you can help others? Create a vision for what you can do to bring more balance, justice, peace, or harmony to our Earth. Your rebelliousness then transforms from a challenge into a gift.

Rejection

The best thing we can do with rejection is to make it a learning experience—rejection is a great teacher.
— Adena Friedman —

Personal Reflections

When my clients come to me feeling the pain of rejection, I can feel their hurt. Wanting to be liked and included is one of our most basic needs. Being accepted first by your family and then by your social group is survival—it's wired into our brains. Research shows that when we feel rejected, the same areas of our brains light up as when we are physically hurt. Ouch.

But I can't just say to them, like in the quote included, "Rejection is a great teacher." That would hurt them even more. Saying that is not acknowledging the pain they are in. It's glossing over their pain with a "lesson." Has anyone ever done that to you? Perhaps when something painful happened to you, was someone's response along the lines of "something good will come from this" or "God doesn't give us anything that we can't handle"? While these may be true in the big picture, in the moment of suffering, these statements usually are not helpful. It feels like a rejection of our feelings.

Writing this helps me understand that there are different kinds of rejection. There can be total rejection of someone or rejection of their thoughts, ideas, beliefs, emotions, or behaviors. They all hurt. Total rejection might hurt the most, but ongoing rejection of someone's thoughts or behaviors might be like death by a thousand cuts—slower but, in the end, just as painful.

Loving Insights

Most beloved and sweet spirits, in your world, you have a game called pinball. Players use levers to hit the balls along a kind of obstacle course. It requires skill to maneuver the ball successfully around the various objects placed in its path. Sometimes the ball gets derailed, and the player needs to begin again. If the player loses a ball, they learn how to maneuver its paths better and then are successful at guiding their ball smoothly around the course to win the game.

As you move around the course of your life, you will encounter some people who are like holes into which the ball falls. Others are like posts or obstacles that knock you off your course or even into the "begin again" channel. Still others redirect the energy into another channel. These people are no more consequential than the posts, holes, or other devices that delay or derail the pinball. They were placed there to be what they are and no more. When you can begin to see that it is not your shortcoming in play here, you will be able to more smoothly direct your energy around the pinball course of life.

When it hurts to feel rejected, acknowledge it then ask to be guided along a smoother path. Put your ball (energy) in play again. Keep clearly in mind what it is you want at the end: the "win" of feeling wanted and included.

When you bounce off one person, that's an indication that your path will be smoother and quicker when you adjust your trajectory a little.

Inspired Actions: Tips and Tools for Transformation

Tips

We see that people may reject us because we don't fit their concept of what they want. As New Age people would say, "Our vibrations don't match." Actually then, they are doing us a favor. If we continued to try to be associated with them, it would be as if we were trying to run AC (alternating current) and DC (direct current) electricity at the same time. That would not work and could even burn out the wires.

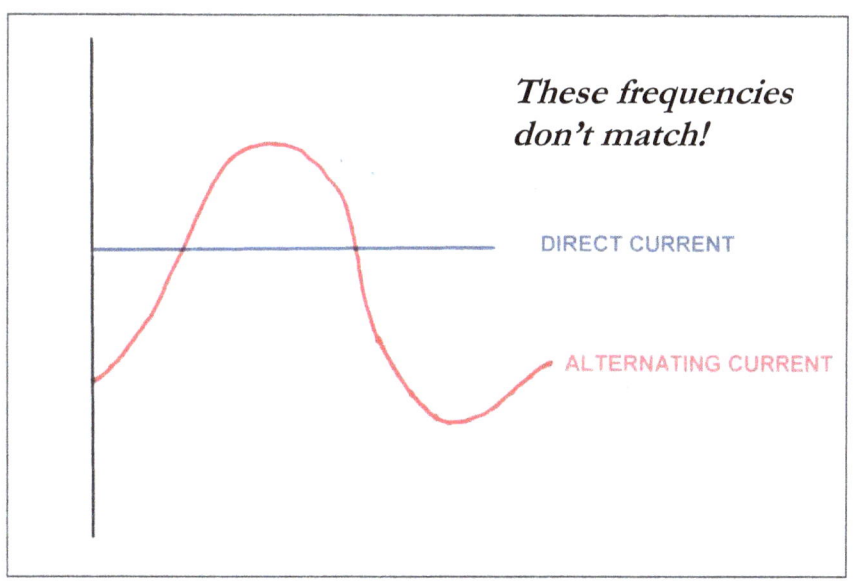

Isn't it much smarter—and easier—to find and associate with people who are on the same or similar wavelength as you?

Tools

My teacher, Billie Topa Tate, has a wonderful exercise to help us feel included and loved. Before you go to a gathering, put your hands on your heart, go inward, visualize the people who will be at that gathering, and internally say, "I love myself; therefore, you love me." Do this at least three times. Then, when you are with the group, you can look at each one and silently say, "I love myself; therefore, you love me (focusing on one person), you love me" (focusing on a second person), and so on. Complete this process by visualizing them saying back to you, "Absolutely, we love you."

Visualization is very powerful—you are creating with your mind. When you steadfastly visualize this, even if the group that has been rejecting you is not able to change their minds, you will begin to find yourself associating with people who accept you and honor you for who you are.

Resentment

*Resentment is like taking poison
and waiting for the other person to die.*
— Malachy McCourt —

Personal Reflections

Have you ever noticed how much energy resentment takes? It is a full-time job to be resentful. Resentment affects your brain and, from there, cascades down through your other bodily systems. It can create a flood of stress hormones that will wear your body down.

Loving Insights

Most beautiful souls, resentment is the acid of relationships and of the mind. Resentment will harden your arteries—both energetic and physical—because resentment flows through each and every thought form. Life is never pleasant when resentment takes up residence in your inner world because resentment eats away at you over and over. It is woven through every cell and every thought and every action. It is a prison from which you cannot easily escape. With resentment, you are reliving the unwanted over and over instead of living it once, learning from it, and moving on. Free yourself now from resentment or, like a vulture consuming the carcass of a deceased animal, it will eat away at you until nothing is left. Once you begin to resent, you are on the path to death. We speak strongly because you must know that to resent is to "resend" the same message to yourself over and over and over. It will burn you out.

What is the antidote for resentment? Over and over, you must take your mind and redirect it to the good in life. While an incident may have occurred that you feel gives you license to resent, you have the choice of reliving it every moment of the day or changing the channel.

When you change a TV channel, the show is still being broadcast; you are just not tuned into that wavelength anymore. You have chosen to watch another station—one that brings you greater happiness. So, too, in your mind; when those old feelings of resentment resurface—and they may because resentment does not like to let go of its grip on you, simply say, "We are changing the channel now." Then redirect your attention to something more pleasing to you. While this may not immediately change an ongoing situation, you certainly will have more pleasure in the moment. String those moments together and you begin to have a new thread of life. Weave those threads together and you have a new tapestry.

Inspired Actions: Tips and Tools for Transformation

Tips

When you break down the word "resentment," it is based on "resent"—so indeed it is you resending the same of negative feelings to yourself over and over. This doesn't sound like very much fun. As the Loving Insights guidance says, change the channel! Surely there is a more interesting program you can tune into.

Emotions: Resentment

As I was writing this section, a poem about resentment came to me. May you find peace with it.

> Ah, resentment, my old friend
> I see you've come to "set" again.
> You hold a grudge, you think you're smart,
> But what you do just hurts my heart.
> You make me feel that I am right
> While those folks there are quite a fright.
> That I am cool is how I feel,
> But that other guy—he's such a heel.
> And I'm "all that," you tell me to think
> While this one here, she's quite the fink.
> We've done this dance, you know it's true,
> But in the end, I just feel blue.
> So now I ask if you'll just go
> And let me be more in the flow
> Of life and how it goes up and down
> Sometimes smile and sometimes frown
> These things that teach me what I need to know
> To make me wise and to help me grow.
> I cannot change anyone's word or deed,
> But I can see it as if it were a seed
> To plant and grow into what I need.
> And I can go where my thoughts roam
> Because my thoughts are just like my home.
> I choose which ones come and which can stay.
> The other ones must go away.
> To keep my house safe and calm
> To soothe my heart just like a balm
> I'm wise about to whom I'll lease,
> And in the end, this gives me peace.

Tools

In hypnotherapy, sometimes we ask the client to imagine the scene they need to process as if it were on a stage or a TV screen. When you do this, you get to be the director! You can send some actors home or offstage, bring in others, or change the script. It is quite amazing how effective this simple technique can be. So, instead of replaying the same scene(s) you have been feeling resentful about over and over, change the script. You don't have to totally rewrite it the first time. Make any little change you'd like. You can put the hurtful scene on an old black-and-white TV then turn that TV off and take it out to the garbage. Now, make a new scene—one more pleasant to you—and see it being played out on a big-screen TV.

Alternatively, you can try these Laughter Yoga exercises.

1. On a large index card or sheet of paper, write or draw the situation in which your resentment began. Fold it in half and set it aside.

2. Now, do this Laughter Yoga warm-up exercise: Stand with your feet about shoulder width apart. Bend down, pick up an imaginary flower, bring it to your nose, and inhale. Do this three times total. This gets your body and imagination going.

3. Next, do this Laughter Yoga exercise, which balances the left and right hemispheres of the brain. Clap your hands together in front of you while saying out loud, "HO HO" (one clap for each "HO"). Then turn to one side and clap three times while saying out loud, "HA HA HA" (one clap for each "HA"). Return to the center and clap twice while saying "HO HO," then turn to the left and clap three times while saying "HA HA HA." Repeat this as many times as feels right to you.

4. Now, pick up the card or sheet of paper on which you wrote or drew your resentment stimulus. Open it and look at what's on it. Now point at it and laugh hysterically as if on it is the funniest thing you've ever seen. Keep laughing until it feels complete.

5. Rip it up and toss the pieces in the air in a shower.

Sadness

*The walls we build around us to keep sadness out
also keep out the joy.*
— Jim Rohn —

Personal Reflections

Sadness—we all have it from time to time. In fact, if we didn't have it, would we be having a fully human experience? Don't we weave the tapestry of life with both light and dark threads? The heavier, darker threads provide the counterpoint for the lighter, brighter ones.

What is sadness all about? Are we evolved if we don't have sadness? Is sadness a choice? Is it a kind of selfishness? Are we sad because we didn't get—or because we lost—something we wanted?

Loving Insights

Sweet ones, the concept of sadness, as you know, is indeed a human concept. In the Heaven world, there is no sadness, for all have a greater understanding of the breadth, the depth, and the transitory nature of life in this realm and other realms. When a soul leaves to partake of an experience in another realm—whether it be on the physical Earth plane or in another vibratory realm—we rejoice for that soul; we know that it is only a matter of time before we are together again. Time is both fast and slow, and we always have the choice to move things around, should we so desire.

On the Earth plane, you feel sad when you do not have your desired condition. You may feel sad if you did not get the job or the mate you wanted. You may feel sad if you had those things and then those things moved on to their next experience. It is understandable; you do not have the same plasticity or fluidity of time and space of which those in the Heaven world are able to take advantage.

As emotions go, sadness is a rather benign one. Who does it hurt? It is not like jealousy or bitterness, which are corroding to the spirit. Sadness is like a soft, gentle rain that falls on the individual. For some, it may rain for longer than for others. Still, the nature of the world is that the rain will cease, and the Sun will come out again.

So, if you can, go out in the rain and fully experience it. Let yourself completely understand what it is to be rained on, to be in the rain, to be with the rain, to be of the rain, and to be the rain. Then mark your calendar for the sunny days ahead. Rain and sun are both necessary, and they alternate depending on the climate where you are. Some people naturally feel more at home in the rainy climates, and that's okay. Others are quite happy to be in the sunny climates, and that's okay.

> **Me:** If someone is feeling sad and wants to be "not sad" again, what should she or he do?

Loving Insights: The best thing to do is first be okay with feeling sad. Sadness comes, and sadness goes. If you try to push it away before its time, you will not succeed. It will be like trying to push water uphill, as they say. Do not add to your burdens with that fruitless exercise.

Instead, find a small moment of peace or even joy. Bring your focus down to the minute. Are you missing your mate, your family, your job, or the life you thought you would have? Step out of that for a moment and bring your focus down to the smallest detail you can find. Look at the petals of a flower. Really look at them. Look even smaller than the petals. Look at the pollen on the stamens. Begin to wonder about that. Wonder what part that pollen plays. Explore the color of the petals. Now start to be one with that flower, with those petals. Let them speak to you, to tell you a story. Perhaps they will even sing to you. Maybe they will give you a poem.

When you are complete with that, you may step back into your sadness. Notice that you just had a few moments of "not sad." That is like a forest clearing. As you journey through the rain forest, you can stop from time to time in this clearing. You can call this clearing to you. You will find that it is available no matter where you go. In those moments, you were not sad.

Inspired Actions: Tips and Tool for Transformation

Tips

I love the idea of bringing your focus down to the minute—that's "minute" as in tiny, but it also could mean "minute" as in a brief amount of time. Either way, we are focusing on the present moment.

Tools

Elizabeth Welles's book, *Women Celebrate: The Gift in Every Moment*, is a collection of essays by women that contains a wonderful essay on bringing your focus down to the tiny details, which the author calls "the Wee of Life." Explore those tiny details and moments, and you will be able to see the wonder through the sadness.

Love yourself. Give yourself a big hug. Pat yourself on the back as you might pat a child when comforting her or him. You don't need words; just hold and pat yourself.

Matt Kahn, a wonderfully practical spiritual teacher, has shared this wisdom: When you feel something like sadness, don't fight it. Just say, "I feel this way because I do, and I'll feel this way until I don't." Isn't this a sweet way to think about it? It takes the pressure off and allows us to just be. Aaahh… can you feel yourself exhaling into peace now?

Self-Empowerment

Whether you think you can, or you think you can't—you're right.
— Henry Ford —

Personal Reflections

My friend Lisa G. seems so self-empowered to me. I am in awe as I witness her design her life. She trained in Kundalini yoga, and during that time, she decided to play the gong—so she did. Then she made a CD of her gong playing—just like that! Next, she bought a harmonium and started to play it. After that, she began writing and singing songs. She followed that up by designing a set of oracle cards and successfully marketing them. She doesn't seem to doubt herself at all. She does whatever she is inspired to do.

Differently, I sometimes—okay, often or almost always—question what I do or should do. For years, people have told me I should write a book. Who, me? A book? About what? What would I have to say that would be of interest to people? This insecurity probably goes back to my childhood when my father would say things like, "That is the stupidest thing you've ever said" or "You don't know what you're talking about." Those demeaning statements went inside me like a shiv and stuck in the place where my self-confidence should have been.

Over time, I learned to overcome that lack of self-empowerment. I got interested in aromatherapy and soon after began to teach classes. Initially, I had hesitations about teaching: Who am I to teach? Don't I need more training? But then I realized that it is up to me, and only me, to make the decision that I am ready and worthy to teach this.

Spirit, what do we need to know about "self-empowerment"?

Loving Insights

You are all children of My Spirit, so in truth, each and every one of you is already self-empowered because you are empowered by Me. The veil of forgetfulness cast over most of humanity is what does not allow you to see this. However, if you pause and allow the outer veils to drift away, you will reconnect internally with All That Is—your true Source and your link to Divinity.

In the human form, self-empowerment can come in many ways. Test yourself—stretch a bit more than you thought you could. Take a class. Learn a skill. Practice speaking more kindly than you have. Empowerment is not just about achievements—that is the outward manifestation of it—which are given much more emphasis in your society. Rather, empowerment is the understanding that you and you alone are in charge of your emotions. When you are empowered, you are not riled by what others say and do. If you temporarily are, you are able to return to balance much more quickly.

For what is more empowering than choosing who and what you want to be in each and every moment? Therefore, look less to the outer and more to the inner. It is here that you will find your empowerment.

Inspired Actions: Tips and Tools for Transformation

Tips

If, while you were growing up, you didn't receive the message that you are self-empowered, you can give it to yourself now. Just like when I realized that no one was going to come along and tell me it is now okay for me to teach aromatherapy, you are the one who can give yourself the "go-ahead" to take positive actions.

If you sometimes think, as I have, that you don't know enough yet, remind yourself of the old adage, "People don't care how much you know until they know how much you care." How much you care is entirely up to you. There is no committee that can give you approval on that!

Remember, too, that we are always evolving. There always will be things we don't know. When we begin to teach or write or whatever we are doing, often someone will ask us something we don't know. In my sales career, I learned that this is a positive because it gives us an opportunity to say, "I'll get back to you on that," and then do so. That second point of connection both shows how much you care and provides another opportunity for you to reach your goal.

Tools

You can have fun creating your self-empowered future with this art project. You will need:

- A box (cardboard is readily available, but you can use any kind)
- Glue or paste
- Pictures cut from magazines, newsletters, and so on

Find pictures that represent the things that have been holding you back from what you would like to do. That might include images of your daily household responsibilities, graphics depicting your fears, illustrations of family pressures, or representations of any other barrier. Paste or glue them onto the inside of the box.

Now find pictures that represent what your life would be like if you felt empowered enough to take the action steps you want. Paste those onto the outside of the box. Voilà! You have just created your new future.

Another fun technique is the NLP (Neuro-Linguistic Programming) Circle of Excellence.

1. In your mind, draw a largish circle on the floor in front of you. Make the circle big enough for you to stand in.

2. Remember a time when you felt the most accomplished, proudest, or happiest with yourself. It might be when you won a contest as a child, got an award at work, or even were praised by someone who mattered to you. If you cannot recall a time when you felt really successful, bring to mind someone who you view as positively self-empowered.

3. Step inside the circle and really BE in that state you were in then. Notice your body standing tall and proud with your shoulders back, your head up, and a big smile on your face. Feel this good feeling in your body, mind, and emotions. If you couldn't remember a situation of your own, imagine that the person you envisioned is in the circle with you and has their hand on your heart, transmitting all those wonderful qualities to you.

4. Step out of the circle and notice any details in the room. (You are taking your mind off the state of excellence to create a break.)

5. Step back into the circle and get right back into that wonderful, self-empowered, successful state.

6. Now, shrink that state up and put it into a small imaginary dot (like a holographic button) somewhere on your body that you can easily and unobtrusively press. This is called an "anchor." Many people like to put that imaginary dot on their hand.

7. Press on that dot/anchor, and you should find yourself feeling that self-confidence as if you had stepped into the Circle of Excellence. If you do not feel it, repeat Steps 2–5 until you have internalized your feelings of self-confidence and self-empowerment, so they come up immediately when you press on your anchor spot.

You may have noticed that I used the word "fun" to describe both exercises in this Tools section. That's appropriate because self-empowerment is best when it's fun! So, go stretch yourself and have some fun.

Susan L. Atchison

Shame

Shame is a soul-eating emotion.
— C. G. Jung —

Personal Reflections

Ahh, Shame, my old friend. Or are you my "frenemy"? I feel like I know you a lot more than I should or than I wish I did. Does it seem odd to you that a person whose life's calling is to be a therapist—and to uplift others—has, most of her life, felt a low level of shame? It was like having an invisible leech attached to me—always there, always sucking out some energy, but never quite noticeable enough to be seen so it could be detached.

For those of you who would like a refresher on the difference between guilt and shame, guilt is feeling bad about something you did (or didn't do) whereas shame is feeling bad about the essence of who you are. Shame can come when someone, instead of correcting a behavior, tells a child that she or he is a "bad" girl or boy. Survivors of abuse also carry the shame their abusers should have. Both psychologically and energetically, abusers tend to transfer their own shame to their victims.

In his book, *Power vs. Force,* David Hawkins created a hierarchy of emotions, from the highest vibration (most empowering) to the lowest vibration (most destructive). He puts the emotion of shame at the bottom. Shame is about as low a feeling as you can have.

For this book, I decided to channel about shame right after I asked about despair. They're kind of partners, don't you agree? When you see shame, despair probably is right there also.

Loving Insights

Behold the power of shame! Shame is used as a tool by those in the know due to its enormous and far-reaching potential. Once you have shamed someone, you easily can gain control over them. They simply wilt; their very being and essence is called into question, and they no longer feel worthy of love or attention. This makes that person easy to manipulate.

Shame has been a tool used for eons to control the masses. Authorities used it, and its use was passed onto teachers and parents. Shame was rampant; it was everywhere, like a bad virus running through a population. It brought everyone down. Even those who thought they were using it to their own ends did not know that they, too, would get infected by it.

Yet the nature of pandemics is that they will run their course and then run out. This, too, will happen for shame. More and more of our beautiful souls are being placed on the Earth to remind others that shame is not a useful tool. It is a boomerang. One by one, people are waking up to the truth that they are not defective. They actually are quite perfect, and each soul is greatly loved. For some, this will be a long journey; for others, it will be like remembering the correct answer to a math problem they knew before they temporarily forgot it.

The essence of shame is slimy gray. You can remove shame simply by asking the Light—the all-giving, all-knowing Light—to penetrate into every nook and cranny of your being—on a cellular and energetic level—and dissolve and vacuum out any and all shame. Ask that this gift also be given to those who have shamed you because they simply did not know any better. When it was started, the users of shame knew better; however, like many old rituals, the meaning and purpose has been lost yet the dry recitation continues. As your grand teacher, Jesus, has said, "Forgive them, Father, for they know not what they do." Forgive them. Forgive them all. Let the healing begin a rolling wave that will cascade across the globe and open a new life for all.

Inspired Actions: Tips and Tools for Transformation

Tips

As a hypnotherapist, I have come to know that shame is held in the body. We can feel it there. Some people feel, sense, or see it as a gray covering or cloud that permeates their body and/or energy field. When you have shame, it affects every part of yourself and your life. Shame often is at the root of addictions, numbing behaviors, and acting out.

Tools

When you want to control anything, one of the first steps is to contain it. We put babies in playpens, animals in corrals, and gardens within fences. A similar technique that can be helpful is to put a container around the shame. This might be easier if the shame is primarily located in one area of your body, but you also can put a container around your entire self. The container serves to create a boundary; the shame is kept inside that boundary. You might envision the boundary or container as a wall, a fence, or even a picture frame.

Next, begin to shrink down the container. Imagine it getting smaller and compressing the shame within it. You may be able to shrink it quite small until it seems doable to simply remove the container and all the shame that's in it. If that's not possible for you right now, just get it as compact as seems right.

You can flush beautiful Light (any color will do—as long as it is bright or pastel and not murky, cloudy, or dark) through the interior of the container as if you were pouring a waterfall through it. Let that waterfall of Light flow through the container until the shame has cleared out.

Another technique is to gradually change the color within the container to a lighter gray. Allow yourself to adjust to this then make it lighter yet again. Continue doing this until the gray is gone entirely then shrink the container down to a tiny dot and zoom it up into the Universe.

Shock

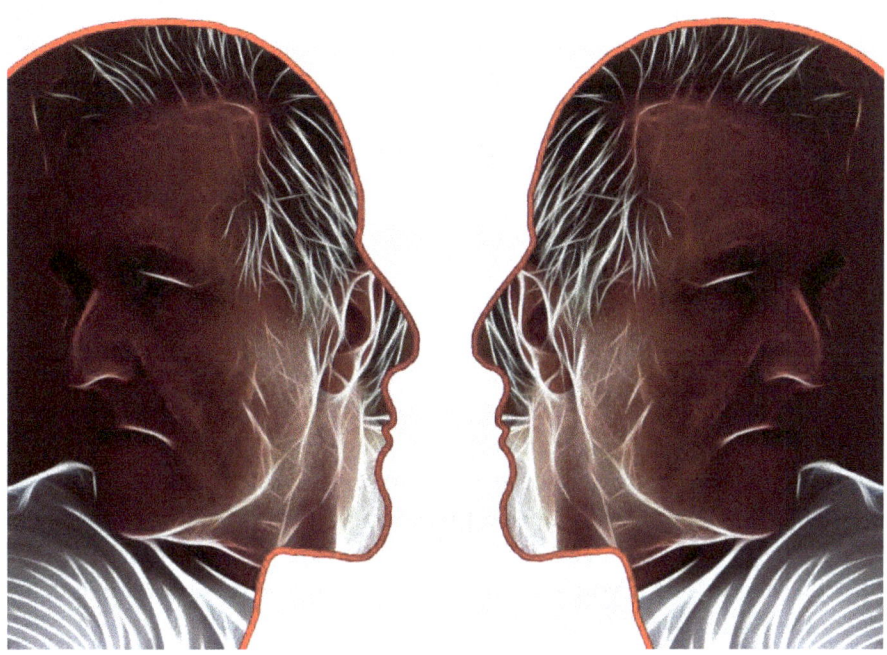

*Sometimes when you're overwhelmed by a situation—
when you're in the darkest of darkness—
that's when your priorities are reordered.*
— Phoebe Snow —

Personal Reflection

What is "shock"? It is the state into which you can go when you are feeling so overwhelmed, with so few resources, that your nervous system gets stuck in fight, flight, or freeze. You might recognize this in yourself or others.

Fight can be seen in someone who wants to fight everyone, whether physically or verbally. They are on the offensive all the time—it's probably a good defense for them. Flight is characterized by a quick exit or the desire to make one. When this is stuck in the "on" position, the person is not really participating in life. He or she is looking for the way out of any situation. Both fight and flight also can be indicated when someone is nervous or agitated, always drumming their fingers on the table or jiggling their foot. Freeze is when the person basically shuts down, goes numb, and is not participating in life. (See section on Numbness.)

Loving Insights

Beloved and beloved and beloved, be aware and be mindful of what you see in others' behaviors. Noticing and understanding their hardwired system will help you create an atmosphere in which you can bring calmness and productive conversation. People on your planet struggle with so much, feeling insecure in so many ways, that they can go on automatic pilot and not truly be present when they are interacting with you. They may not even know that they are presenting a shell of themselves. It is as if you are interacting with a false cardboard front that they are holding up.

You may not be able to heal them just by knowing this, but what you can do is avoid being caught up in the energetic vortex of their overwhelm. Energy is attracted to like energy, and if the person you are with is in a state of shock, this easily could set off the similar energy in your situation. It is a survival mechanism.

In times of war, it was an advantage for the fight energy to be easily transmitted to everyone nearby. It could save their lives. Most of you are fortunate enough not to be in a warlike situation, but someone in a fight mode is. If you can recognize that as simply a physical and energetic response in which they are stuck, you can remember to breathe in your own sense of calmness, thus defusing it for yourself at least. And who knows, you might defuse it in them a bit as well.

Inspired Actions: Tips and Tools for Transformation

Tips

If you are the one who is experiencing shock, it can be helpful simply to have it named. Shock is your body's way of attempting to discharge the adrenaline your body requested when you felt under attack. Sort of like an oil spill, if you don't do something to clean it up, the effects just stay there and pollute everything.

Tools

Holding something hot or cold can be helpful to soothe shock. Often, warmth is good for the freeze response while cold is ameliorating for the fight and flight responses. However, it's good not to assume which shock it is. If you are experiencing the shock symptoms, test it out. If it's another person, ask what would feel better for them—to hold something warm or something cool. Warmth can be provided by a cup of hot tea or a towel heated in the microwave. Coolness can be given through an iced drink or the gel packs you put in the freezer.

Essential oils can go right to the amygdala—the part of the brain that begins the fight/flight response and processes emotions. Inhaling lavender is very soothing; rosemary is stimulating.

Simple breathing techniques also are helpful. If you are feeling numb, hold your left nostril closed (the easiest way is to use your ring finger on the outside of the left nostril) and breathe in and out through the right nostril. This is energizing. If you are agitated, put your thumb on the outside of your right nostril to hold it closed and breathe in and out through your left nostril only. This is calming. Try three rounds of inhale and exhale then pause to assess how you feel. If you need it, try another three rounds and so forth.

If it feels safe for the person, a soft touch is healing here, too. Humans are wired to respond to caring from another. Safe touches are physically, emotionally, and energetically healing.

Susan L. Atchison

Worthiness

*Our stresses, anxieties, pains, and problems arise because
we do not see the world, others, or even ourselves as worthy of love.*
— Prem Prakash —

Personal Reflections

Feeling worthy must be interconnected with every one of the other emotional states discussed in this book. A true, healthy sense of self-worth makes it easy to be patient and have empathy, compassion, and joy. On the other hand, a lack of self-worth is often at the root of fear, anger, depression, despair, and so forth.

Loving Insights

Indeed, wondrous ones, while all souls are created worthy, some souls get "beaten up" by life on the Earth plane and begin to lose their sense of divine worthiness. People can be born with an inner sense of worth only to have it weakened or destroyed by the behaviors of those around them. People also can be born with a faulty sense of self-worth due to experiences they have had in their past lives. Some things take a while to recover from.

At the heart, though, each soul has been created by (and is part and parcel of) the Creator, so each soul intrinsically is worthy. All the rest is like a cloud of dust that has covered the purity of the soul.

If your feelings of a lack of self-worth come from the words and actions of those around you, remember that what they say and do actually has very little to do with you. It is them acting out their own play of life. As best as you can, allow that to wash off you. Imagine a clear stream of living light washing through the deepest levels of you, lifting up and carrying off the dust and grime created by hurtful words and actions. See it also filling in the empty places with sparkling Light, healing and regenerating you.

If your feelings of low self-worth come from your own actions in this or a prior life, give yourself some understanding and love. Ask for forgiveness and make restitutions as best as you can, even if they are symbolic. You are demonstrating to yourself that you are righting the ship and intend to sail it in a beautiful, course-corrected line from now on.

Inspired Actions: Tips and Tools for Transformation

Tips

If you have been feeling a lack of worthiness, dedicate yourself to lifting yourself up. Every day, sit in meditation. Close your eyes and slow your breath. The mind follows the breath. Look inside yourself with the intention of finding the pure gold center of Light that glows—the seed that contains your essence. You may see, sense, feel, or know it is there.

If you are not able to see, sense, feel, or know, then just imagine. If you cannot imagine, then pretend you can imagine. Like a small ember in your mind, blow gently on the golden seed. Imagine it beginning to glow a little brighter and become a little larger.

Tools

You might like to use the beginning of the Invocation to the Unified Chakra:

> I breathe in Light
> Through the center of my heart,
> Opening my heart
> Into a beautiful ball of Light,
> Allowing myself to expand.

Doing this over and over will begin to expand your sense of self. As you go through your day, look for synchronicities; be aware of the beauty of the world. Do your best to bring happiness and light to others. When you lay your head on the pillow at night, give thanks for another day. Ask that you be guided and assisted in the nighttime work done by your energy body or that you be guided to the Temple of Healing to heal all unworthiness so you can bring the gift of a true self back to the world.

Susan L. Atchison

Recommended Resources

Creative and Compassionate Life (art, journaling, meditation, ritual, storytelling, webinars, and programs)

- Elizabeth Welles's website: www.elizabethwelles.com
- *Unfathomable Podcast*: www.UnfathomablePodcast.com
- *How to Rest in 4 Easy Steps*: www.elizabethwelles.com/howtorest/
- *Journaling for Well-Being & Peace* by Elizabeth Welles: www.amazon.com/Journaling-Well-Being-Peace-Elizabeth-Welles/dp/0974399817/

Crystals

- *Jewel of the Lotus: Tibetan Gemstone Oracle* by Dawn Silver: www.amazon.com/Jewels-Lotus-Tibetan-Gemstone-Oracle/dp/1885394330

Essential Oils

- To learn more or purchase therapeutic-grade essential oils: www.oilson.org

Grounding

- *Grounding: Exploring Earthing Science and the Benefits Behind It*: www.healthline.com/health/grounding/

Loneliness Felt as Physical Pain

- *Social isolation, loneliness can cause serious physical pain*: www.grandchallenges.ucla.edu/happenings/2016/12/21/social-isolation-loneliness-can-cause-serious-physical-pain/
- *Loneliness actually hurts us on a cellular level* by Brian Resnick www.vox.com/science-and-health/2017/1/30/14219498/loneliness-hurts

Meditation and Chanting

- Susan leads online Meditation and Chanting programs on the fourth Saturday of each month from 4–6 p.m. CT. For more information or to register, go to www.ahealingsoul.com/meditation-and-chanting

Nutritional Focus

- **Detoxing and nutritional plans:** Anthony Williams, the "Medical Medium," has several easy-to-read books offering his higher perspective on nutrition:
    - Website: www.medicalmedium.com
    - Facebook group: www.facebook.com/groups/medicalmediummembers/
- **Testing:** Pfeiffer Medical Center specializes in the assessment and management of biochemical imbalances.
    - Website: www.hriptc.org/index.php

Psychological

- Brené Brown is a research professor at the University of Houston who holds the Huffington–Brené Brown Endowed Chair. For two decades, she has studied courage, vulnerability, shame, and empathy. She is the author of five #1 *New York Times* bestsellers: *The Gifts of Imperfection*, *Daring Greatly*, *Rising Strong*, *Braving the Wilderness*, and *Dare to Lead*, and has done several TED talks.
    - Website: www.BreneBrown.com
    - TED talks
        - Listening to Shame: www.brenebrown.com/videos/ted-talk-listening-to-shame/
        - The Power of Vulnerability: www.brenebrown.com/videos/ted-talk-the-power-of-vulnerability/
- Byron Katie
    - *Loving What Is, Revised Edition: Four Questions That Can Change Your Life* with Stephen Mitchell: www.amazon.com/Loving-What-Revised-Questions-Change/dp/0593234510
    - Website: www.thework.com
- *The 12 Stages of Healing: A Network Approach to Wholeness* by Donald M. Epstein with Nathaniel Altman: www.amazon.com/12-Stages-Healing-Approach-Wholeness/dp/1878424084

Sleep Deprivation

- *Sleep Deprivation & Loneliness:* https://healthiersleepmag.com/sleep-deprivation-loneliness/

Spiritual: Healers/Teachers

- **Amma Sri Karunamayi** is a Hindu spiritual leader who travels internationally promoting global peace and meditation. www.karunamayi.org
- **Billie Topa Tate** is a Native American Mescalero Apache healer and intuitive found at the Mystical Sciences Institute Healing Wellness Center in Evanston, IL; 847-866-0505; www.msi-healing.com
- **Matt Khan** is a spiritual teacher.
  - *Whatever Arises, Love That: A Love Revolution That Begins with You*: www.amazon.com/Whatever-Arises-Love-That-Revolution/dp/1683644697
  - *Everything Is Here to Help You: A Loving Guide to Your Soul's Evolution*: www.amazon.com/Everything-Here-Help-You-Challenges/dp/1401954979/
  - *The Universe Always Has a Plan: The 10 Golden Rules of Letting Go*: www.amazon.com/Universe-Always-Has-Plan-Letting/dp/1401965253
  - Website: www.mattkahn.org
  - Facebook: www.facebook.com/mattkahn/

Spiritual: Intuition Training

- The Voice for Love, founded by Candace and DavidPaul Doyle: www.thevoiceforlove.com
- *5 Steps to Hearing God's Voice: For Those on the Leading Edge of Consciousness* (Author's Edition): www.amazon.com/5-Steps-Hearing-Gods-Voice/dp/1937621006/
- Facebook: www.facebook.com/thevoiceforlove

Spiritual: Kundalini Practices

- 3HO: A World of Kundalini Yoga: www.3HO.org
- Spirit Voyage: www.SpiritVoyage.com

Spiritual: Resources

- **Aramaic Lord's Prayer:** An internet search of this term will yield the Aramaic version; you are likely to find a variety of translations of Aramaic into English.

Spiritual: Resources (continued)

- **Channeled Book**: *Ask and It Is Given: Learning to Manifest Your Desires* by Esther and Jerry Hicks: www.amazon.com/Ask-Given-Learning-Manifest-Desires/dp/1401904599

- **Niscience:** This means Knowing, an archetypal system of spiritual instruction received by Ann Ree Colton for students of the higher life. The Talisman exercise is given in *The Anointed* by Ann Ree Colton and Jonathan Murro of the Ann Ree Foundation of Niscience, Inc., 1987. www.niscience.org

Niscience Thought Talisman Exercise

There are left-hand and right-hand ways of thinking. Inverted thought is the left-hand way of thinking; creative thought is the right-hand way of thinking. The Niscience student seeks to transpose his thought into the right-hand way of thinking or creative thought. In inverted or left-hand thinking, thought works in cycles of repetition. In right-hand thinking, thought works in rhythms of recapitulation. For example, in inverted thinking the senses use the law of repetition through which a person is painfully taught day by day. In creative thought, the soul, working with rhythmic recapitulation, continues to return certain creative and spiritualized ideas, until, through dedication, the mind becomes receptive to these greater and immortal ideas. Inverted thought sets up a chain of circumstances that dominates the habit patterns of life. Thus, he who would work creatively with the spiritual or higher aspects of the mental triad atoms should begin now to organize the ebb and flow within his thoughts.

V. MORNING REFLECTION EXERCISE (10 DAYS)

For best results in organizing the thought, it is recommended that the student briefly reflect upon the words in Chart 2 in the morning hours. This morning reflection should consume no more than ten minutes, and should be observed only in the morning. He should reflect upon the words dispassionately and without concentration. And he should continue this visualizing and illumining morning reflection exercise for a period of ten days, so that he may begin his works of transforming grace through thought. If the student finds it necessary in the future, he may return to this morning reflection exercise. (Only Chart 2 is to be used for the morning exercise. It is recommended that one read the left-hand inverted thought, and speak aloud with deep feeling and receptivity the right-hand thought.)

Chart 2

Inverted or Left-Hand Thought	Creative or Right-Hand Thought	Inverted or Left-Hand Thought	Creative or Right-Hand Thought
Accusing	Relinquishing	Infidelity	Fidelity
Aggressive	Peace-giving	Judging	Charitable
Bitter	Non-resentment	Lustful	Reverent
Covetous	Sharing	Manipulative	Acceptance
Fiery-concentration	Mediation	Non-believing	Open-minded
Combative	Patient	Non-cooperative	Joy in creation
Complacent	Interested	Painful	Healing
Critical	Forgiving	Possessive	Impersonality
Cunning	Magnanimous	Prejudiced	Spiritual justice
Doubt	Faithful	Proud	Humble
Disloyal	Loyal	Crude-psychical	Spiritual
Egotistical	Non-claiming	Regretful	Joyous
Fearful	Fearless	Repelling	Compassionate
Frigid	Warming	Resisting	Peaceable
Greed	Giving	Rigidity	Pliant
Guilt thoughts of the past	Appreciation for the blessings of today	Sterile	Receptive
		Stubborn	Flexible
Hateful	Loving	Subtle	Pure
Hopeless	Hopeful	Suspicious	Trustful
Hostile	Hospitable	Timid	Courageous
Indecisive	Purposeful		

Photo Credits

Acceptance photograph by **John Hain/johnhain**

- Photograph sourced from www.pixabay.com/illustrations/love-kindness-meditation-1221449/
- For more work by John Hain, go to www.johnhain.com or www.pixabay.com/users/johnhain-352999/

Anger photograph by **Dr StClaire/Matryx**

- Photograph sourced from www.pixabay.com/illustrations/anger-angry-gamer-gaming-5043564/
- For more work by Matryx, go to www.pixabay.com/users/matryx-15948447/

Anxiety photograph by **Stefan Keller/KELLEPICS**

- Photograph sourced from www.pixabay.com/photos/fantasy-spirit-nightmare-dream-2847724/
- For more work by KELLEPICS, go to www.pixabay.com/users/kellepics-4893063/

Avoidance photograph by **John Hain**

- Photograph sourced from www.pixabay.com/illustrations/signs-desire-avoid-positive-1172208/
- For more work by John Hain, go to www.johnhain.com or www.pixabay.com/users/johnhain-352999/

Belonging photograph by **congerdesign**

- Photograph sourced from www.pixabay.com/photos/heart-cord-suspended-love-together-1450300/
- For more work by congerdesign, go to www.pixabay.com/users/congerdesign-509903/

Betrayal photograph by **Gerd Altman/geralt**

- Photograph* sourced from www.pixabay.com/illustrations/puzzle-trust-reliability-certainty-2515123/
- For more work by Gerd Altman, go to www.pixabay.com/users/geralt-9301/

*Original photograph slightly modified by Susan L. Atchison

Bitterness photograph by **PollyDot**

- Photograph sourced from www.pixabay.com/photos/prisoner-sculpture-280274/
- For more work by PollyDot, go to www.pixabay.com/users/pollydot-160618/

Bliss photograph by **Mohamed Hassan/mohamed_hassan**

- Photograph sourced from www.pixabay.com/photos/sunset-dawn-nature-dusk-sun-sky-3128170/
- For more work by Mohamed Hassan, go to www.pixabay.com/users/mohamed_hassan-5229782/

Compassion photograph by **Gerd Altman/geralt**

- Photograph sourced from www.pixabay.com/illustrations/face-head-empathy-meet-sensitivity-985982/
- For more work by Gerd Altman, go to www.pixabay.com/users/geralt-9301/

Criticism photograph by **Gerd Altman/geralt**

- Photograph sourced from www.pixabay.com/photos/bullying-woman-face-stress-shame-3096216/
- For more work by Gerd Altman, go to www.pixabay.com/users/geralt-9301/

Depression photograph by **kerttu**

- Photograph sourced from www.pixabay.com/photos/graveyard-sculpture-woman-cemetery-523110/
- For more of kerttu's work, go to www.pixabay.com/users/kerttu-569708/

Despair photograph by **Richard Mcall/Richard MC**

- Photograph sourced from www.pixabay.com/photos/grief-loss-missing-reclining-lady-2584778/
- For more work by Richard Mcall, go to www.pixabay.com/users/richardmc-1834381/

Photo Credits

Determination photograph by **Nadja Donauer/nadjadonauer**

- Photograph sourced from www.pixabay.com/photos/resilience-sunflower-enforce-nature-4159761/
- For more work by Nadja Donauer, go to www.pixabay.com/users/nadjadonauer-2905787/

Disappointment photograph by **Shaarc/PixArc**

- Photograph sourced from www.pixabay.com/photos/sad-broken-glass-sadness-597089/
- For more work by PixArc, go to www.pixabay.com/users/pixarc-692595/

Empathy photograph by **Gerd Altman/geralt**

- Photograph sourced from www.pixabay.com/illustrations/face-head-empathy-meet-sensitivity-985977/
- For more work by Gerd Altman, go to www.pixabay.com/users/geralt-9301/

Emptiness photograph by **Gerd Altman/geralt**

- Photograph sourced from www.pixabay.com/photos/head-skull-blow-resolution-resolve-2709732/
- For more work by Gerd Altman, go to www.pixabay.com/users/geralt-9301/

Faith photograph by **Gerd Altman/geralt**

- Photograph sourced from www.pixabay.com/photos/clouds-landscape-beyond-sky-rays-2709662/
- For more work by Gerd Altman, go to www.pixabay.com/users/geralt-9301/

Fear photograph by **John Hain/johnhain**

- Photograph sourced from www.pixabay.com/illustrations/fear-emotion-anxiety-vulnerability-2083653/
- For more work by John Hain, go to www.johnhain.com or www.pixabay.com/users/johnhain-352999/

Forgiveness photograph by **svklimkin/klimkin**

- Photograph sourced from www.pixabay.com/photos/hand-gift-bouquet-congratulation-1549399/
- For more work by svklimkin, go to www.pixabay.com/users/klimkin-1298145/

Fulfillment photograph by **Ami/Aquamarine_song**

- Photograph sourced from www.pixabay.com/illustrations/heart-wings-flame-star-light-3519858/
- For more work by Ami, go to www.pixabay.com/users/aquamarine_song-4143828/

Gratitude photograph by **Nina Edmondson/NinaMarie**

- Photograph sourced from www.pixabay.com/photos/sign-positive-gratitude-inspiration-2432252/
- For more work by Nina Edmondson, go to www.ninaedmondson.com or www.pixabay.com/users/ninamarie-5460906/

Greed photograph by **Gerd Altman/geralt**

- Photograph sourced from www.pixabay.com/illustrations/more-flame-fire-brand-burn-better-687241/
- For more work by Gerd Altman, go to www.pixabay.com/users/geralt-9301/

Grief photograph by **Richard Mcall/Richard MC**

- Photograph sourced from www.pixabay.com/photos/grave-graveyard-cemetary-milan-3165597/
- For more work by Richard Mcall, go to www.pixabay.com/users/richardmc-1834381/

Guilt photograph by **Gerd Altman/geralt**

- Photograph sourced from www.pixabay.com/photos/guilty-finger-suggest-3096217/
- For more work by Gerd Altman, go to www.pixabay.com/users/geralt-9301/

Photo Credits

Hopelessness photograph by **Ulrike Mai/Counselling**

- Photograph sourced from www.pixabay.com/photos/holzfigur-stones-life-struggle-980784/
- For more work by Ulrike Mai, go to www.pixabay.com/users/counselling-440107/

Impatience photograph by **S. Hermann / F. Richter/pixel2013**

- Photograph sourced from www.pixabay.com/photos/girl-time-time-pressure-worried-2786277/
- For more work by S. Hermann / F. Richter, go to www.pixabay.com/users/pixel2013-2364555/

Inspiration photograph by **Gerd Altman/geralt**

- Photograph sourced from www.pixabay.com/illustrations/silhouette-woman-meditation-165530/
- For more work by Gerd Altman, go to www.pixabay.com/users/geralt-9301/

Jealousy photograph by **Zorro4**

- Photograph* sourced from www.pixabay.com/photos/sculpture-dragon-stone-horticulture-1346988/
- For more work by Zorro4, go to www.pixabay.com/users/zorro4-796252/

Joy photograph by **Silvio Zimmermann/bugent**

- Photograph sourced from www.pixabay.com/illustrations/balloons-spring-nature-watercolour-1615032/
- For more work by Silvio Zimmermann, go to www.pixabay.com/users/bugent-3155975/

Judgment photograph by **John Hain/johnhain**

- Photograph sourced from www.pixabay.com/illustrations/insecurity-judgment-relationship-1767736/
- For more work by John Hain, go to www.johnhain.com or www.pixabay.com/users/johnhain-352999/

*Original photograph slightly modified by Susan L. Atchison

Laziness photograph by **Karsten Paulick/Kapa65**

- Photograph* sourced from www.pixabay.com/photos/animal-sloth-close-up-sleep-tree-1622007/
- For more work by Karsten Paulick, go to www.pixabay.com/users/kapa65-61253/

Loneliness photograph by **Manfred Antranias Zimmer/Antranias**

- Photograph sourced from www.pixabay.com/photos/person-woman-girl-alone-409127/
- For more work by Manfred Antranias Zimmer, go to www.pixabay.com/users/antranias-50356/

Love photograph by **Gerd Altman/geralt**

- Photograph sourced from www.pixabay.com/illustrations/candle-light-bill-heart-love-luck-67851/
- For more work by Gerd Altman, go to www.pixabay.com/users/geralt-9301/

Numbness photograph by **Alicja/_Alicja_**

- Photograph sourced from www.pixabay.com/photos/leaf-snow-season-cold-frozen-4766033/
- For more work by Alicja, go to www.pixabay.com/users/_alicja_-5975425/

Oneness photograph by **Gerd Altman/geralt**

- Photograph sourced from www.pixabay.com/illustrations/woman-silhouette-meditation-clouds-1927662/
- For more work by Gerd Altman, go to www.pixabay.com/users/geralt-9301/

Rage photograph by **Gerd Altman/geralt**

- Photograph sourced from www.pixabay.com/illustrations/cry-person-face-abstract-banner-1682140/
- For more work by Gerd Altman, go to www.pixabay.com/users/geralt-9301/

*Original photograph slightly modified by Susan L. Atchison

Photo Credits

Rebelliousness photograph by **Lisa Runnels/Greyerbaby**

- Photograph sourced from www.pixabay.com/photos/hands-words-meaning-fingers-423794/
- For more work by Lisa Runnels, go to www.pixabay.com/users/greyerbaby-2323/

Rejection photograph by **Ben Kerckx/Ben_Kerckx**

- Photograph sourced from www.pixabay.com/photos/birds-decoration-figurines-276191/
- For more work by Ben Kerckx, go to www.pixabay.com/users/ben_kerckx-69781/

Resentment photograph by **Arek Socha/qimono**

- Photograph sourced from www.pixabay.com/illustrations/poison-bottle-medicine-old-symbol-1481596/
- For more work by Arek Socha, go to www.pixabay.com/users/qimono-1962238/

Sadness photograph by **Lisa Runnels/Greyerbaby**

- Photograph sourced from www.pixabay.com/photos/girl-walking-teddy-bear-child-walk-447701/
- For more work by Lisa Runnels, go to www.pixabay.com/users/greyerbaby-2323/

Self-Empowerment photograph by **Colin Behrens/ColiN00B**

- Photograph sourced from www.pixabay.com/photos/light-bulb-idea-creativity-socket-3104355/
- For more work by Colin Behrens, go to www.pixabay.com/users/colin00b-346653/

Shame photograph by **hannahlmyers**

- Photograph sourced from www.pixabay.com/photos/statue-art-sculpture-metal-5235587/
- For more work by hannahlmyers, go to www.pixabay.com/users/hannahlmyers-4637214/

Shock photograph by **Gerd Altman/geralt**

- Photograph sourced from www.pixabay.com/photos/face-faces-dialogue-talk-psyche-65058/
- For more work by Gerd Altman, go to www.pixabay.com/users/geralt-9301/

Worthiness photograph by **S. Hermann / F. Richter/pixel2013**

- Photograph sourced from www.pixabay.com/illustrations/yoga-meditation-buddha-yin-and-yang-1915564/
- For more work by S. Hermann / F. Richter, go to www.pixabay.com/users/pixel2013-2364555/

Acknowledgments

My Family

To my husband, Woody, who is my own in-house Zen Guru. Despite never having studied (in this life, anyway!) any spiritual teachings and, truth be told, not really believing in them, he unfailingly maintains a cheerful attitude (to me, he is the funniest man alive); sees the best in others; never has a bad word to say about anyone or anything; does not take offense, easily lets things go; and always is friendly, kind, helpful, and nurturing to people and animals. I think that if we passed away more or less at the same time, and if there is a St. Peter at the gates of Heaven, Woody would be at the front of the line to be let in just because of who he is and the goodness woven through his entire life. Plus, as he often reminds me, he once gave $1.00 to a street preacher who then told Woody that he was saved. So, it's all taken care of.

To my sister, who also does not have any interest at all in most of my studies yet still supports me in everything I do and is especially good at giving special dispensation whenever I call her to say that I've gone shopping and have spent too much.

To my Italian in-laws, who taught me how to hug, how to love, and almost as importantly, how to make escarole soup.

To Lisa Selby, who, although not technically related to me, is the "daughter of my heart." I like to say that we "met by chants." Lisa teaches me every day about how to live and love unconditionally and exuberantly. Thank you, Lisa, for who you are. Lisa is the artist and creator of the beautiful lotus that is used for the Inspired Actions exercise in the Acceptance section.

My Teachers

To Billie Topa Tate, Native Mescalero Apache healer and teacher, who has given me many gifts of spiritual practices. Perhaps one of her greatest gifts is her essence. While one of the most advanced spiritual teachers I've known, she also is one of the most genuinely humble. Billie truly lives to serve.
To Amma Sri Karunamayi, the embodiment of the Divine, who brings the lesson of kindness and compassion to all of her "children."

To David Hartman, Diane Zimberoff, and Yvonne Christman, who gave me some of my early training in hypnotherapy, altered states, and subtle energies. You introduced me to chanting and opened my life in ways that I never could have envisioned.

To Matt Kahn, whom I've not yet met, but who inspires me with his sweet and heart-centered teachings.

My Friends

To Elizabeth Welles, a multitalented author, artist, actor, and singer. Your honest feedback and support helped these writings become the best that they could be.

To Jean Haner, who knows fate brought us together in college. We lost touch for a while afterward, and when we reconnected, we discovered that we had independently pursued similar paths. Jean is the author of books on space clearing, face reading, and using the five elements to balance and improve your life. I learn something every time I read anything she has written.

To Lisa Gniady, my friend, colleague, fellow intuitive, and companion to Bali and India. You always encouraged (okay, pushed) me to get my own work out there. Thank you.

My Clients

To all my clients who have trusted me to be by their side while they have gently explored the roots of their wounds. I am humbled to have been a witness while they have grown upward through watery emotions to blossom in the sunlight.

My Editor

To Victoria Hyla Maldonado of Victorious Editing Services, who so adeptly handled the editing, formatting, and publishing of this book. She had me at "I'm incredibly intrigued by this project." Victoria understood the concept of these writings and beautifully fine-tuned the wording while staying true to its essence. At each step, she explained her suggested changes and was open to my ideas. Together, we collaborated to make the best choices. Plus, Victoria totally raised the bar in terms of response and turnaround time. She is Super Editor Woman, faster than a speeding keyboard, more powerful than problematic punctuation, and able to leap over dangling participles in a single bound.

Susan L. Atchison

About the Author

Susan L. Atchison is the founder of A Healing Soul, Ltd. (located in the Chicago suburbs), which is dedicated to the healing of deep, difficult, or stuck issues. She has been practicing holistic counseling since 1999.

Susan has studied and trained extensively in the areas of human thought, emotion, and behavior as well as in energetic and spiritual dynamics. She has masters of arts degrees in Communications and Counseling Psychology, is a licensed clinical professional counselor in the State of Illinois, and has earned certifications as an advanced clinical hypnotherapist, neuro-linguistic programming practitioner, breathwork release therapist, and aromatherapist. In addition, she has trained in Akashic Records reading, clearing negative energy from people and spaces, Reiki master teaching, Reiki cranial fascia, grief and trauma, the polyvagal approach, and Roger Woolger past life therapy. She also has studied and worked with shamanic and subtle energy healing, including past life, interlife, pre- and peri-natal (rebirthing), gestalt, psychodrama, soul retrievals, spirit releasement (clearing elementals, entities, aliens, thought forms, and other energy attachments), and shadow work.

Susan's approach is about giving people their own space to heal, to be comfortable with and compassionate about whatever they may need to share. She believes that this era is one in which people are taking back their own power and that the deepest, most powerful and complete healing happens when you reach inside and heal yourself.

Susan understands what it is to be human (with all our weaknesses and strengths). She understands that people want to be well; that dysfunctional emotions or behaviors are simply attempts to take care of ourselves in the only ways we know at the time; and that, given support, people can rediscover their strengths and possibilities for growth.

Susan loves to meditate and chant, listen to harmonious music and also be immersed in beautiful silence, create gardens, provide a sanctuary for birds and other wildlife, and laugh.

If you enjoyed this book, feel free to follow Susan on Facebook at www.facebook.com/AHealingSoul/.

Personalized Loving Insights Message

Would you like your own personalized Loving Insights message? You can visit www.lovinginsights.com/messages to make your purchase.

A Loving Insights intuitive message is a way to open your perspective to a wider wisdom on your life by helping you see the beauty and balance woven through even a seemingly difficult time.

When you purchase a Loving Insights message, you will receive a personalized intuitive message from the Higher Realms. Your personal message, which typically is both uplifting and focused on what is most important for you to understand at this time will come to you in writing via email.

If you have questions about your message, you are welcome to connect with me for a follow-up Sharing Session at www.lovinginsights.com/product/sharing-session.

www.ingramcontent.com/pod-product-compliance
Lightning Source LLC
Chambersburg PA
CBHW050144170426
43197CB00011B/1952